The Spirit of Invention

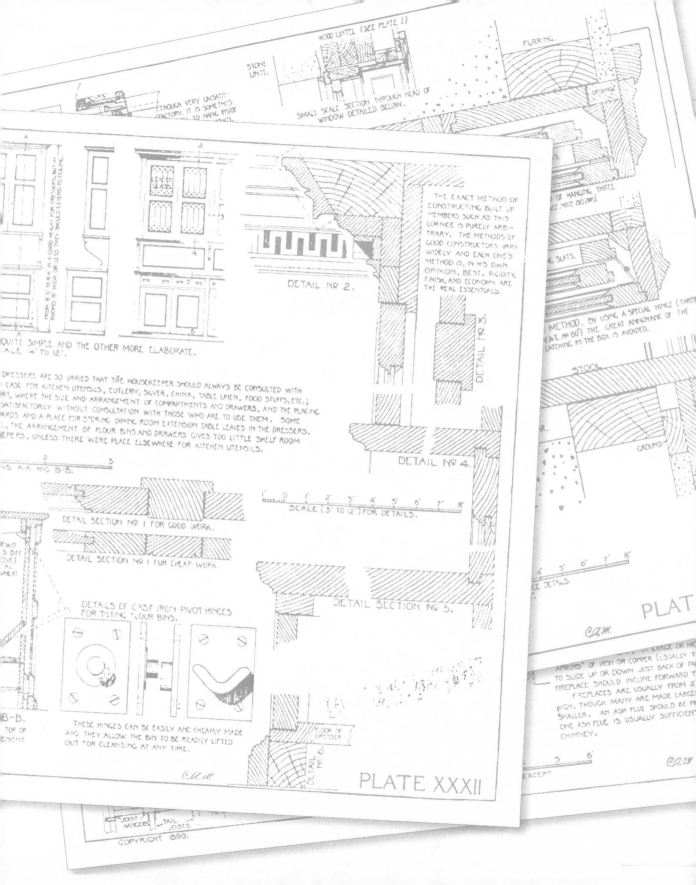

THOUGH VERY UNSATIS-
FACTORY, IT IS SOMETIMES
... TO HANG INSIDE

WOOD LINTEL (SEE PLATE I)

STONE
LINTEL.

SMALL SCALE SECTION THROUGH HEAD OF
WINDOW DETAILED BELOW.

FURRING.

GROUND

THE EXACT METHOD OF
CONSTRUCTING BUILT UP
MEMBERS SUCH AS THIS
CORNICE IS PURELY ARBI-
TRARY. THE METHODS OF
GOOD CONSTRUCTORS VARY
WIDELY AND EACH ONE'S
METHOD IS, IN HIS OWN
OPINION, BEST. RIGIDITY,
FINISH, AND ECONOMY ARE
THE REAL ESSENTIALS.

DETAIL Nº 2.

DETAIL Nº 3.

DETAIL Nº 4.

... OF HANGING, THREE
... NOTE BELOW).

... SLATS.

METHOD. BY USING A SPECIAL HINGE (THIRTY
... Nº 60) THE GREAT ANNOYANCE OF THE
... CATCHING IN THE BOX IS AVOIDED.

STOOL

GROUND

QUITE SIMPLE AND THE OTHER MORE ELABORATE.
...ALE ... TO 12'.

...DRESSERS ARE SO VARIED THAT THE HOUSEKEEPER SHOULD ALWAYS BE CONSULTED WITH
...CASE FOR KITCHEN UTENSILS, CUTLERY, SILVER, CHINA, TABLE LINEN, FOOD STUFFS, ETC.;
...RT, WHERE THE SIZE AND ARRANGEMENT OF COMPARTMENTS AND DRAWERS, AND THE PLACING
...SATISFACTORILY WITHOUT CONSULTATION WITH THOSE WHO ARE TO USE THEM. SOME
...ARDS AND A PLACE FOR STORING DINING ROOM EXTENSION TABLE LEAVES IN THE DRESSERS.
..., THE ARRANGEMENT OF FLOUR BINS AND DRAWERS GIVES TOO LITTLE SHELF ROOM
...KEEPERS, UNLESS THERE WERE PLACE ELSEWHERE FOR KITCHEN UTENSILS.

...S A-A AND B-B.

DETAIL SECTION Nº 1 FOR GOOD WORK.

DETAIL SECTION Nº 1 FOR CHEAP WORK.

SCALE (3' TO 12') FOR DETAILS.

DETAIL SECTION Nº 5.

DETAILS OF CAST IRON PIVOT HINGES
FOR TILTING FLOUR BINS.

THESE HINGES CAN BE EASILY AND CHEAPLY MADE
AND THEY ALLOW THE BIN TO BE READILY LIFTED
OUT FOR CLEANSING AT ANY TIME.

B-B.
...TOP OF
...MENT

C.A.M.

PLATE XXXII

PLAT...

C.A.M.

... IN LARGE OR HI...
APRONS OF IRON OR COPPER (USUALLY T...
TO SLIDE UP OR DOWN JUST BACK OF FA...
FIREPLACE SHOULD INCLINE FORWARD T...
FIREPLACES ARE USUALLY FROM 2...
HIGH, THOUGH MANY ARE MADE LARGE...
SMALLER. AN ASH FLUE SHOULD BE P...
ONE ASH FLUE IS USUALLY SUFFICIENT...
CHIMNEY.

C.A.M.

JOIST
HANGERS
TAIL
JOISTS

COPYRIGHT 1899.

THE SPIRIT OF INVENTION

··

The Story of the Thinkers, Creators,
and Dreamers Who Formed Our Nation

Julie M. Fenster

In Association with the Lemelson Center for the Study of Invention and Innovation
National Museum of American History, Smithsonian Institution

An Imprint of HarperCollins*Publishers*
HARPER www.harpercollins.com

Smithsonian Books

HarperCollins books may be purchased for educational, business, or sales promotional use. For information, please write: Special Markets Department, HarperCollins Publishers, 10 East 53rd Street, New York, NY 10022.

FIRST EDITION

Designed by Kris Tobiassen

Library of Congress Cataloging-in-Publication Data has been applied for.

ISBN: 978-0-06-123189-6

09 10 11 12 13   OV/QW   10 9 8 7 6 5 4 3 2 1

For Frederick Allen
and the great old days
when he was the editor par excellence
of *American Heritage of Invention & Technology*

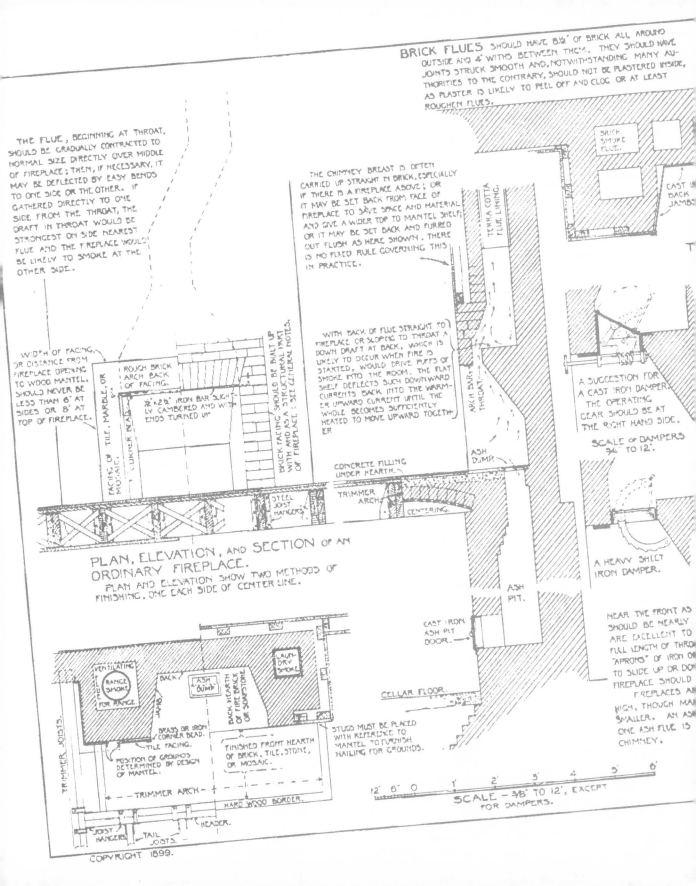

BRICK FLUES SHOULD HAVE 8½" OF BRICK ALL AROUND OUTSIDE AND 4" WITHS BETWEEN THEM. THEY SHOULD HAVE JOINTS STRUCK SMOOTH AND, NOTWITHSTANDING MANY AUTHORITIES TO THE CONTRARY, SHOULD NOT BE PLASTERED INSIDE, AS PLASTER IS LIKELY TO PEEL OFF AND CLOG OR AT LEAST ROUGHEN FLUES.

THE FLUE, BEGINNING AT THROAT, SHOULD BE GRADUALLY CONTRACTED TO NORMAL SIZE DIRECTLY OVER MIDDLE OF FIREPLACE; THEN, IF NECESSARY, IT MAY BE DEFLECTED BY EASY BENDS TO ONE SIDE OR THE OTHER. IF GATHERED DIRECTLY TO ONE SIDE FROM THE THROAT, THE DRAFT IN THROAT WOULD BE STRONGEST ON SIDE NEAREST FLUE AND THE FIREPLACE WOULD BE LIKELY TO SMOKE AT THE OTHER SIDE.

THE CHIMNEY BREAST IS OFTEN CARRIED UP STRAIGHT IN BRICK, ESPECIALLY IF THERE IS A FIREPLACE ABOVE; OR IT MAY BE SET BACK FROM FACE OF FIREPLACE TO SAVE SPACE AND MATERIAL AND GIVE A WIDER TOP TO MANTEL SHELF; OR IT MAY BE SET BACK AND FURRED OUT FLUSH AS HERE SHOWN. THERE IS NO FIXED RULE GOVERNING THIS IN PRACTICE.

TERRA COTTA FLUE LINING.

BRICK SMOKE FLUE.

CAST I... BACK JAMB...

WITH BACK OF FLUE STRAIGHT TO FIREPLACE OR SLOPING TO THROAT A DOWN DRAFT AT BACK, WHICH IS LIKELY TO OCCUR WHEN FIRE IS STARTED, WOULD DRIVE PUFFS OF SMOKE INTO THE ROOM. THE FLAT SHELF DEFLECTS SUCH DOWNWARD CURRENTS BACK INTO THE WARMER UPWARD CURRENT UNTIL THE WHOLE BECOMES SUFFICIENTLY HEATED TO MOVE UPWARD TOGETHER

ARCH BAR, THROAT.

A SUGGESTION FOR A CAST IRON DAMPER. THE OPERATING GEAR SHOULD BE AT THE RIGHT HAND SIDE.

SCALE OF DAMPERS ¾ TO 12".

WIDTH OF FACING, OR DISTANCE FROM FIREPLACE OPENING TO WOOD MANTEL, SHOULD NEVER BE LESS THAN 6" AT SIDES OR 8" AT TOP OF FIREPLACE.

ROUGH BRICK ARCH BACK OF FACING.

FACING OF TILE, MARBLE, OR MOSAIC.

CORNER BEAD.

½"×2½" IRON BAR SLIGHTLY CAMBERED AND WITH ENDS TURNED UP.

BRICK FACING SHOULD BE BUILT UP WITH AND AS A STRUCTURAL PART OF FIREPLACE. SEE GENERAL NOTES.

CONCRETE FILLING UNDER HEARTH.

ASH DUMP.

TRIMMER ARCH.

STEEL JOIST HANGERS.

CENTERING.

A HEAVY SHEET IRON DAMPER.

PLAN, ELEVATION, AND SECTION OF AN ORDINARY FIREPLACE.
PLAN AND ELEVATION SHOW TWO METHODS OF FINISHING, ONE EACH SIDE OF CENTER LINE.

ASH PIT.

CAST IRON ASH PIT DOOR.

CELLAR FLOOR.

NEAR THE FRONT AS... SHOULD BE NEARLY... ARE EXCELLENT TO... FULL LENGTH OF THRO... "APRONS" OF IRON O... TO SLIDE UP OR DO... FIREPLACE SHOULD... FIREPLACES A... HIGH, THOUGH MA... SMALLER. AN AS... ONE ASH FLUE IS... CHIMNEY.

TRIMMER JOISTS.

VENTILATING FLUE FOR RANGE.

RANGE SMOKE FOR RANGE.

BACK.

ASH DUMP.

LAUNDRY SMOKE.

JAMBS.

BACK HEARTH OF FIRE BRICK OR SOAPSTONE.

BRASS OR IRON CORNER BEAD.
TILE FACING.

POSITION OF GROUNDS DETERMINED BY DESIGN OF MANTEL.

FINISHED FRONT HEARTH OF BRICK, TILE, STONE, OR MOSAIC.

STUDS MUST BE PLACED WITH REFERENCE TO MANTEL TO FURNISH NAILING FOR GROUNDS.

TRIMMER ARCH.

HARD WOOD BORDER.

JOIST HANGERS.

TAIL JOISTS.

HEADER.

SCALE – 3/8" TO 12", EXCEPT FOR DAMPERS.

12 6 0   1   2   3   4   5   6'

COPYRIGHT 1899.

CONTENTS

FOREWORD

*W*hen I first met inventor Jerome Lemelson in 1994, the main thing I noticed was that his mind was constantly churning out ideas and offering solutions. I have vivid memories of walking with him through the Smithsonian's National Museum of American History, where he not only appreciated the displayed inventions for their historic value, but also engaged with them directly, suggesting a better design, for example, or another way the inventor could have solved the same problem. Even history was not safe from his critical gaze, making me wonder how Alexander Graham Bell might have reacted to his suggestions for improving the telephone. But Jerome Lemelson did far more than critique the inventions of others.

Jerry, as he was known to his friends and family, began his own inventing career after serving in the Army Air Corps engineering department in World War II and completing a bachelor's and two master's degrees in engineering at New York University. A decisive moment came in 1951 while he was visiting a factory in Brooklyn, where he observed the operation of a punch-card-controlled metal lathe. This awakened him to the possibilities of automated industrial machinery, and he began work on plans for a universal robot that could measure, weld, rivet, transport, and even inspect. A major breakthrough was his introduction of "machine vision," whereby the robot used computers to analyze digitized images from a video camera. This basic idea laid the foundation for a forty-five-year inventing career, culminating in over six hundred patents, one of the highest totals in American history. Ranging far and wide, his patents went beyond industrial technologies to include toys, recording apparatus, medical devices, and more, and his inventions were incorporated into products such as the camcorder and the cordless telephone.

While he began his career working for corporations, he soon struck out on his own as an independent inventor, often facing overwhelming odds. He always believed that individuals could succeed if they worked hard and had faith in themselves. He became known as a champion of fellow independents, especially the "little guy" inventors, men and women alike.

Guided by this belief, he and his wife, Dorothy, began the Lemelson Foundation to support inventors and invention around the world. The Smithsonian's Lemelson Center, which opened in 1995 as one of their beneficiaries, is a product of this same universal spirit of invention. Our mission is to explore the central role of invention and innovation in the history of the United States. This book grows out of the Lemelson Center's commitment to bringing the stories of invention to popular audiences who may have had little prior exposure to that history.

Jerry Lemelson used the international recognition that he achieved to raise awareness of the work of all inventors. In that spirit, this book highlights the legions of lesser-known individuals whose inventions have permeated our daily lives in ways great and small. Julie Fenster gives us a tantalizing glimpse into the successes—and failures—not of mythical figures, but of real inventors who have shaped our world. We dedicate *The Spirit of Invention* to those readers who are curious about what makes inventors tick and how invention has shaped the history of the United States.

ARTHUR P. MOLELLA

Jerome and Dorothy Lemelson Director
Lemelson Center for the Study of Invention and Innovation
National Museum of American History
Smithsonian Institution

PREFACE

*I*n modern times, industrial times, bottom-line-thinking sorts of times, invention is commonly mistaken for its rapacious cousin, entrepreneurship. The person who is shown something innovative feels compelled to cut right to what seems to be the point and cast judgment according to the signal standard of entrepreneurship: did it make money?

In point of fact, invention has been around a lot longer than entrepreneurship. It's certainly been around longer than money. Money, after all, was somebody's bright new idea once. And there were long eras of human invention before that.

When I was invited to write a book on the spirit of invention, I was wary that the expectation on the part of the readers might be for yet another rendition of the usual gaggle of "successful" inventors: Cyrus McCormick, Eli Whitney, Robert Fulton. I have nothing against any of those inventors, but I do have a grudge against history that reinforces convenient distortions, such as the idea that great inventors are famous inventors—and vice versa. And that invention is but a stepchild of business. The result of such thinking is that a few storied names, such as those above, have entered into a realm akin to folklore, there to define the art of invention in American history, while leaving the impression that only a measured number of rather exalted people have been outstanding in the field. That impression is wrong.

Both invention and entrepreneurship attempt to effect a change. The two certainly share something of the same impetus: to fill a need, where only a blank existed before. Whatever the overlap, however, the difference is far more telling. While entrepreneurship is born of competition in civilization—the more complex, the better—invention is innate to humans as individuals.

Crows possess the knack of invention, designing tools to achieve whatever end they may have in mind. Some spiders are likewise unbound by mere instinct, as are several primate species. Invention, however, is more than just an occasional necessity for human beings; it is an impulse that helps to define the species. It emerges in the individual as a reaction to the splendid frustration of one's surroundings, as well as one's uncharted potential, a response as basic in most people as having children: to leave a mark and give a gift, perchance for the better, to the future.

Any number of the people in this book failed, but only on the post-invention end. They invented brilliantly, yet created items that did not make any lasting impact in general use: here, they are celebrated for their moment of invention. A great inventor is not necessarily a good entrepreneur, after all, or even a passable one. No matter. It is the universal experience of the inventor and the sheer courage of innovation that is the topic at hand.

Some of the people in this book are now lost to history in every respect save one, signing their lives not with names but only with inventions still in use today. How can we see a person who is no longer there? Through the solution he or she left to a problem he or she felt compelled to solve. The well-remembered Thomas Edison, on the other hand, is included not for any object that he patented but rather for the concept of the research laboratory, which he first introduced on a grand scale at Menlo Park, New Jersey. Considered as an invention, one copied by thousands across the globe, the research lab had more impact than anything else in his output. No less significant an example of the inventing impulse is revealed in the story of Frank Hill, who went into the West Virginia coal mines as a child. At sixteen, he saw one of his friends crushed in a sudden cave-in. Hill spent the next thirty years creating a warning device, thinking it through by the hour in a lab no bigger than the notebook he always carried with him. Once he was finally ready, he built a prototype that was tested and heartily endorsed by his state's mining administrator. Before Hill's device could be properly introduced, though, it was obviated by new mining methods. Yet Hill is no less a great inventor than Edison in that he answered the compulsion to innovate and made something that worked. That is the spirit of invention.

This book looks at the life of the inventor, first in a chronological way and then from the perspective of the inventive mind, which uses the senses to cultivate the possibilities of the world. An amalgamation of experiences, it features a set of great inventors, most of whom have never been mentioned in any book (or on the Internet). They bring remarkable stories, and each lends a snapshot of that moment before other complications encroach, when the spirit of invention is all that there is, inborn and irresistible.

The Life of an Inventor

Little children invent—and while it is true that some of those hailed as prodigies happen to have parents in the business of inventing or of securing patents, it is also true that the spirit of invention is ageless. Kids can surprise anyone with their cleverness, and so can their most ancient elders. The five chapters that follow chart the ways that invention flowers at different points over the course of a life span. As talent emerges, families encourage it, colleges nurture it, and corporate laboratories nervously wait for it.

Armies have always sought out the latest advantage, but in modern times, nations have come to depend on innovation for position in economic wars as well as military ones. The inventor is part of a new philosophy of government. When problems arise, it isn't the rousing leadership and blind faith of previous eras that calm widespread fear. As of the twenty-first century, the trust of the populace lies with invention. The U.S. government has thrived on the shift in priority, becoming the greatest single incubator of innovation, with its laboratories employing tens of thousands of active inventors.

The rise of organized invention has not sent the independent inventor to oblivion, but it has offered a steady livelihood for those with the ability to remain independent even in harness. It's a demanding trick, but one with its own rewards. Inventing, once a treacherous gamble of time and effort, has become a wholly sober career choice.

The chapters that follow present a running biography, moving with the years to reflect the emergence of the spirit of invention in anyone, at any time. Over the course of a lifetime, as can be seen, an inventor grows through stages set out by others—or else barges straight through them on a path with no markings.

THE SPIRIT OF INVENTION

CHAPTER ONE

Who Is an Inventor

I n the spring of 1880, a professor in Ohio was working on the process behind an invention he named the Automatic Indicator. A later age would call it text messaging. "The invention in many respects resembles a pocket compass," explained a description of the day. When the needle on one Indicator, arrayed with the alphabet all the way around the rim, was turned from letter to letter, the needle on a twin device moved in kind. Such devices had been known since the 1830s, but never before had they been wireless. People equipped with the professor's Automatic Indicators could purportedly send each other messages from different blocks, different cities, and even different time zones. Someone who had visited the professor would say only that the secret lay in the power of magnetics.

In Fredericksburg, Virginia, a retired army general named Daniel Ruggles was devoting his free time that same spring to experiments with balloons and explosives. Ruggles had commanded a cannon brigade at Shiloh during the Civil War, timing his offensives to avoid the

The ABC telegraph that Charles Wheatstone patented in 1858 worked in a fashion similar to the Automatic Indicator.

View of Union soldiers on the ground holding tether lines while Professor Lowe ventures aloft in the balloon *Intrepid* during the Battle of Fair Oaks, May 31 and June 1, 1862. Balloons were used for aerial reconnaissance during the war.

rainstorms that were never far away during the two-day battle. In 1880, Ruggles was still annoyed by the fact that not even a general can give orders to a cloud—and expect a response. He invented a heavily armed balloon that could be detonated when it was in the midst of a cloud and thereby shake loose a rainstorm.

All in all, it was just another season of ideas in America. In Albany, New York, a young woman named Skerritt was in consultation with the Delaware & Hudson Railroad. That year, D&H passengers were stepping on and off trains neatly and safely by way of the fold-down steps that Miss Skerritt had invented especially for railroad cars. In Auburn, Indiana, during the same span, Henry N. Staats was usually to be found on one body of water or another, demonstrating his revolution in rowboating, which promised nothing less than the removal of the rowing. Instead of hauling on oars, a person cranked a propeller. It was said to be very easy, and even if it wasn't, Staats had a remedy for aching arms. He included a pin in the works that reversed the direction of the propeller, allowing the operator to continue going forward by cranking in the opposite direction, "which is often a great relief to the muscles." Either that or, if the pin slipped, the boat went backward.

John McAdams was out on the water, too, but in Boston Harbor. He had cultivated a thought about applying brake power to ocean liners, and he was trying it out in the real world—the real world of dinghies, that is. Then rafts, then a friend's launch, and finally a side-wheel steamboat. McAdams' niece had once been aboard a ship involved in a collision, watching with hundreds of other passengers as the two ships sped inexorably toward each other, the respective officers having no way to stop or quickly change course. McAdams, a machinist by trade, fashioned what he called "fins" that were to be clamped by way of hinges to the sides of a ship. When a lever on deck released them, the force of the water flung them outward. With that, the drag-coefficient of the ship did an immediate flip-flop and the vessel stopped short as though it were at the end of a leash. On the day of McAdams' test in the harbor, the side-wheel steamboat jolted from full speed (twelve miles per hour) to a dead stop in the space of just ten feet.

In Indianapolis, a man with the remarkably inaccurate name of Albert Fearnaught was working on his own original invention: a means to allay the terror of being inadvertently buried alive. His system relied on a means of communication with the outside world and included an air circulation system, which could be activated from underground. In Philadelphia, another inventor was stoically confronting an even more odious dread: the smell of sauerkraut cooking on the stove. "The louder it smells, the better the kraut," ran a cheery saying of the day. The Philadelphian was experimenting with various antidotes, worn under the nose on a pad of his own design.

Across the country, people were, as ever, busily turning flights of imagination into metal and wood—or, in the case of General Ruggles' inventory of supplies for his rainmaking apparatus, into "metallic wire, textile fibre, cordage and elastic tubes." In the first year or two of the 1880s, Ruggles was only one among the millions loose in the laboratory of modern America, thinking out ways to make it even more modern. With or without patents, people were crafting fins for ships, stairs for trains, and pads for their noses.

Nonetheless, there are those who would argue that the natural leaning of history is toward an account of success, not of failure or even of benign, peripheral obscurity. In that vein, the attitude toward invention, in particular, is prone to hero worship of a select few. People who don't even know what a cotton gin is know that Eli Whitney invented it. Good reasons undoubtedly present themselves for whittling the expansive world of invention down to a few storied names. The deeper understanding of technology can be a struggle for those outside a particular specialty, and anyway, practically everyone craves a triumphant story.

And yet, if the study of the history of technology demonstrates anything, it is only that—evidently—nobody ever invented anything. That's the impression left by the general scramble to claim priority in the wake of a widely hailed invention. Throughout the nineteenth century, suspicion was rampant that Whitney, a northerner, had taken the idea for his cotton gin from some resident of the South during his sojourn there in 1792–93: Catherine Greene, proprietress of the Georgia plantation that Whitney was visiting at the time; Sam, one of the slaves working on the place; or the owner of another plantation in the region. No proof was ever found that Whitney was not the originator of his cotton gin, but many people nonetheless found it hard to believe that a person who had never before set eyes on the notoriously stubborn short-staple cotton plant could possibly invent a machine to make it part with its seeds.

Eli Whitney

This photo depicts a replica of Whitney's original model, c. 1840. It is not accurate; the handle is attached to the wrong shaft.

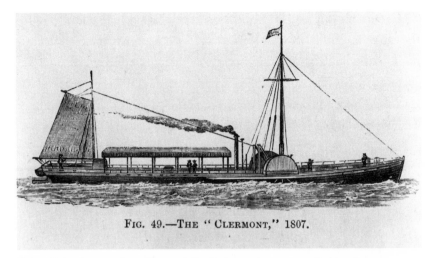

Fig. 49.—The "Clermont," 1807.

Robert Fulton's steamboat *Clermont*, the first vessel ever propelled by steam.

Robert Fulton, another archetype, drew even more skeptics, yet his reputation as the inventor of the steamboat has been impervious to them all. In 1802, he was encouraged by a New York investor to look into the idea of a riverboat propelled by steam power. As the prospective inventor of the steamboat, he had an unusual advantage. He had already seen one in operation—perhaps even two. Neither had caught on, but in a famous demonstration in 1807, Fulton's version did prove its worth. That immediately placed him at the hub of an even more reliable machine, one that produced people claiming to have originated the steamboat. They came forth throughout the rest of the nineteenth century.

No one leapt to claim credit for the sauerkraut defense system. Or the rowless rowboat. Yet they were as important as the mighty steamboat in conception, if not in influence. The true story behind any single invention eventually leads to all others, making the history of technology an overwhelming tangle of interdependent, crisscrossing ideas.

Band saw, c. 1910.

Even amid the tangle, with its endless relationships blatant or untraceable, inventing is ultimately as individual as any creative effort. It represents a kind of tangible optimism, present in everyone who has ever found an inventive solution to an everyday problem: curbing the smoke coming into a room from the fireplace with a tinfoil scoop or keeping the filling of a half-finished pie in place with a wedge of bent metal. Despite resolving about twice per week to take out a patent on one advance or another, the average homespun inventor rarely files any papers. The same has been true throughout the history of invention: some of the most ingenious inventions are simply anonymous.

The band saw, a dynamic breakthrough of the 1860s, had a direct antecedent in the sash saw of colonial times. The sash saw was an anonymous invention, a long blade constructed as part of a frame that held

Modern-day sash saws. In colonial times, sash saws were long blades constructed as part of a frame that held raw timber in place for cutting, powered by a water wheel.

raw timber in place for cutting. Powered by a water wheel, it was a welcome improvement over hand-sawing in terms of human effort, but it was slow. It was also inefficient, wasting a lot of wood that it turned into sawdust with its thick strokes. There was always more wood, though, in colonial times, and generally there was plenty of time. Anyway, for all of its drawbacks, the sash saw was easy to use.

As the pace of demand for lumber grew, the circular saw was invented, first by an anonymous inventor in Europe in the late 1700s. In 1813 a Massachusetts woman named Tabitha Babbitt originated the same idea on her own. Thinking that she had priority, she refused patent protection and offered the circular saw to the world. It was not the great gift that it might have seemed. The power available in mills at the time couldn't turn a very large saw, and since a circular saw can't cut anything wider than its own radius, the early models couldn't handle thick timber. Many mills were forced to continue using a straight saw. By the 1840s, though, the pace of the industry had accelerated past the sash saw, which seemed more cumbersome than ever and slow. By the end of the decade, someone came along to save the day (a great many of them, in fact) by inventing the so-called muley saw, which was simpler and quicker than the sash saw, relying on a pair of cunning guides, rather than a box frame, to hold a straight line against the timber. The only clue to the identity of the inventor is that he or she may have been born in Germany, since the word *muley* comes from the German word *Sägemühle* (sawmill). Aside from that, the inventor can only be seen in the long reach of his or her idea.

A muley saw was lighter and simpler than a sash saw, relying on a pair of cunning guides, rather than a box frame, to hold a straight line against the timber.

"It is sometimes said that the progress of the present age is the result of invention," said a prominent minister at the end of the nineteenth century. "It is a great deal nearer the truth to say that invention comes from the spirit and need of the age. Can the mere invention of a machine make a people great and prosperous unless they have and recognize a need of it?" He surmised, by way of example, that native peoples without a written language wouldn't suddenly become great literary artists if one among them happened to invent the typewriter. At the same time, he might also have wondered why his own era wasn't ready for the Automatic Indicator, even if it could have been made to work (and for all we know, it did somehow work). The majority of his fellow citizens weren't in quite such a hurry though; not yet—not for instant messages.

A Perpetual-Motion Machine

For over a thousand years, inventors have fallen prey to the dream of perpetual motion. The proposition seems simple enough: a mechanical device, properly constructed, will recycle an initial input of energy and power itself indefinitely. Water will rush from vessel to vessel without stopping; wheels will turn round and round unceasing. One of the first to suggest such a machine was a Flemish architect named Villard de Hennecourt in the 1200s. By the mid-1800s, however, physicists had cast a shadow over the notion of perpetual motion. They defined the Second Law of Thermodynamics, which stated in part that "in all energy exchanges, if no energy enters or leaves the system, the potential energy of the state will always be less than that of the initial state."

Nothing could have been clearer. The law said it couldn't be done—which did nothing to stop the dogged inventors who have been trying to build perpetual-motion machines ever since.

In some cases, the result has been tragic. A German mechanic in New York devoted twenty-five years to construction of his machine, carefully packing it and taking it with him whenever he moved. Even when he lost his job, he was glad, because it meant he could work on his invention full-time. Finally, though, he lost his battle with the laws of physics. "Mary," he said to his wife, "I think I'll have to give it up. It's no use. I can't think it out anymore." Later in the week, he hanged himself from a crossbar on his machine.

Perpetual motion is invariably a tease and a frustration for its believers. Whether based on weights, water, or some other construct, the typical machine comes close to success—tantalizingly close—but falls just short. For that reason, the quest for perpetual motion has turned many an inventor into a con artist, attracting investors and then, success being so very near, twisting more money out of them, year in and year out. (Needless to say, it has turned more than a few con artists into self-described inventors as well.)

The effort to build a perpetual-motion machine reflects what is best and worst about the inventing spirit—and the human one. Erick Johnson was an eighty-six-year-old farmer in northwestern Minnesota. He couldn't read or write, but he did understand the rudiments of machinery. A friend from Sweden confided in him the "secret" of perpetual motion: that a machine based on interlocking wheels would turn indefinitely if someone could build and balance it just right. Johnson spent twenty years trying. "It's equipment shortage what's tying me up now," he said in 1973. "I ordered them inner tubes weeks ago and haven't got them yet. But I think they could be it." Perhaps he was wrong about perpetual motion and inner tubes and everything scientific, but Erick Johnson had greatness in him, too. He was moved by the same pulse as the most brilliant inventors on earth, and he expressed it more simply than any.

"People tell me it won't work," he said of his idea. "But maybe it will."

In the sawmills, emerging ideas were likewise encouraged or distorted by the backdrop of history, that is, by rising expectations.

While a muley saw could cut thick timber, it wasted wood. But then, so did the circular saw, which destroyed five-sixteenths of an inch of wood along its track. In earlier times, timber was cheap and no one particularly cared how much of it went onto the floor in the form of sawdust. By the middle of the nineteenth century, though, wood was actually scarce in many areas formerly covered by forestland. Sawyers couldn't afford to sacrifice their hardwood to circular or muley saws, and they actively looked for an alternative. If one couldn't be found, then the price of furniture and even plain lumber would climb steeply, just when the country was ready to grow, building western cities and homes for an influx of immigrants.

The band saw edged onto the scene, but it wasn't received as an instant miracle. To most sawyers, it looked more like a bundle of problems. Anyone who could look past them, however, saw the potential. The band saw employed a blade so thin that it could be joined into a circle, as though it were a belt. The idea had been patented in England in 1808, but it wasn't until a Frenchman devised a way to join the ends of the band securely that the new saw became somewhat practical. Turning along two wheels, it was known for precision. In cutting veneers, it reduced the track from the circular saw's five-sixteenths of an inch to a mere one-twelfth of an inch. Even so, the band saw was still an unfinished machine. "The application of the principle," observed the historian Rodney Loehr, "depended upon the solution of a complex of technical difficulties. Nearly two decades were to pass in the solution of these problems before the band mill could become a practical reality. Some improvements had to await developments in other industries."

The increasing value of trees presented the many inventors associated with the band saw not only with the last step—demand for a working machine—but with the first as well. It posed a crucial question, which is what any invention exists to answer. In the case of Eli Whitney's first visit to the South, the question was already out in the open; people had

Band saw, c. 1880

been trying to invent a gin for short-staple cotton for sixty years before Whitney heard guests talking about it at a dinner party. In other, less felicitous, cases, inventors have been hobbled by the first step: matching their talents with the right question and framing it to leave the widest chance of success.

An Indiana sawmill owner named Jacob Hoffman led efforts in the United States to develop the band saw's capacity beyond veneers into the brutish work of cutting logs. He took out a total of four patents on subassemblies or tools relating to such problems as the band tension and alignment of the wood. Through his efforts, in conjunction with those of other people, the tool was continuously improved. By about 1870, the band saw was in common use in mills, palpably extending the nation's forest resources. Where the circular saw of that time left 312 feet of every 1,000 board-feet of lumber on the floor as sawdust, the band saw lost only 83 feet.

As in the case of the vast majority of great inventions, the band saw's development was not a neatly packaged tale of one exciting day, but rather a story of myriad days and many triumphs of invention. Such projects bind inventors together, for all of their competitive spirit. Jacob Hoffman didn't invent the band saw, yet he was part of it. Perhaps it invented him in a way, a man drawn forward by each new development on "the big Saw," as he called it.

Just as there are steps common to the development of an invention, there are phases in the life of an inventor: means of honing the instinct into a habit and the habit into a discipline. The fact that innovation may then bring a living is not as revealing of the person or the human race as the fact that it was, in any case, already a way of life.

 **CHAPTER TWO**

Aunt Orinda

FAMILY AND CHILDHOOD

The Great Depression was only one of Gertrude Forbes' problems. A Nova Scotian by birth, she had been sickly since childhood, moving to southern California for the sake of her health in the 1920s. A frail and rather tiny woman, she settled down happily for a while, marrying a railroad clerk, but the warm weather didn't cure her ills. At the age of forty-two in 1933, Mrs. Forbes was bedridden, suffering heart problems. A year later, her husband died. Without any steady income, she had to move into a roominghouse—and not a very posh one, at $7 a month.

Before long, Forbes couldn't afford even her cheap room and so, with nowhere else to go, she accepted an invitation to live rent-free in her aunt's attic. No longer bedridden, though hardly robust, she took stock of her prospects. There was no money to speak of, never more than a few dollars at any given time. Nor did she have any connections or job experience. The world, including most of her relatives, had long since given up on her as she sat in her attic room by the hour, gathering the strength to go downstairs.

Forbes' total assets amounted to just one: an eye for invention. "My family was waiting to call the undertaker," she later said, "all except Aunt Orinda. She had faith in my ideas." Invention can start anywhere, but it is nurtured in the home, for children or adults. With the outside world blowing a fog of discouragement over newly arriving creative people of all types, an inventor needs an Aunt Orinda, "a believer," as Henry Ford called his wife, Clara. With barely a penny, Gertrude Forbes started the Forbes Specialty Company in the mid-1930s. "My own brother called me crazy," she recalled. "But not Aunt Orinda. She'd say, 'Gertrude, you keep on working on your ideas. Some day you'll make good.'"

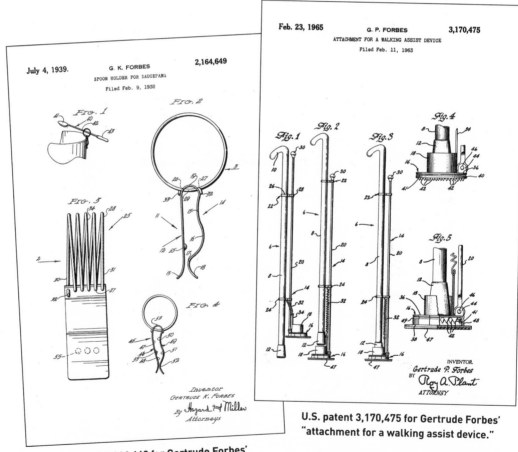

U.S. patent 2,164,649 for Gertrude Forbes' clamp that attached a spoon to a pot.

U.S. patent 3,170,475 for Gertrude Forbes' "attachment for a walking assist device."

Forbes started by designing a purse with fifteen compartments to keep small items organized, and she also worked diligently on a clamp that attached a spoon to a pot, so that it would always be handy for stirring. That idea later proved valuable enough that she had to go to court to defend her patent. In the mid-thirties, however, Forbes' existence was guided by a stark equation: sell at least a few spoon clamps during the day or go without dinner. She sometimes fainted, either from hunger or from debilitation. Nonetheless, she had no intention of allowing her physical problems to stop her. She had a harder time, though, persevering in the face of a daily dose of animosity. As she recalled, people would routinely call her a crackpot or ask rudely why she didn't get a job.

Forbes Specialty finally had a success in the late 1930s with Forbes' invention of an adjustable ironing board cover. The first time she showed one to a department store buyer in Los Angeles, she received an order for two dozen of them. Arriving home in triumph, she couldn't pause to celebrate. Instead, she had to borrow $5 so that she could buy material and make the covers. Eventually, Forbes' ironing board covers were made by a team of employees and were sold all over the world.

"It was always in my soul to design and create," Gertrude Forbes later said. "I guess that's what kept me from taking an ordinary job—that and Aunt Orinda." She sold the company for a sizable sum in 1953 and, remarrying, announced that she was retiring from inventing. It didn't prove possible though. As Gertrude Forbes Heintzelman grew into her seventies—an age no one had expected her to see before she founded her company—she needed help walking. So it was that in 1963, the U.S. Patent Office approved her application for an "attachment for a walking assist device."

H. C. Haynes had been born to former slaves in Alabama around 1870. Going to work as an errand boy at the age of ten, he ultimately earned his living as a barber. In that heyday of the straight razor, a barber would clean and sharpen the blade by brushing it back and forth on a long piece of leather called a strop. The hypnotic swing of the razor against the strop was one of those ceremonies that made the old-time tonsorial a relaxing place for a man, whether he actually needed a shave or not. Haynes knew his profession well, and he thought it absurd that barbers made their own strops, often very badly, by cutting apart old horse harnesses. In the mid-1890s, Haynes built a strop laboratory—most surely the world's first—in the back of his barbershop in San Francisco. As time permitted, he experimented with both the leather and the hardware that attached the strop to the wall. Eventually, he invented a model strop: better for the blades as well as for the barbers, since it was ready to use right out of the package.

Most barbers at the time were white, and Haynes didn't have much success selling his strops to them because of the racial prejudice of the 1890s. Haynes was not an easy man to deter, however. He placed ads in magazines and sold his new strop through the mail. Suddenly, he had orders for thousands of them. Haynes was stunned. The avalanche of orders was overwhelming and could easily have spelled the end of the improved strop. Hayne's wife, Louise, however, was not about to let her husband fail after all that he'd been through; she turned the first floor of their home into a factory and started turning out strops.

Whether inventors require more encouragement as children or as adults, survival and success are typically cultivated by someone at home. Some inventors, it is true, give their families more cause for panic than praise. As a professor at the Massachusetts Institute of Technology, Harold "Doc" Edgerton perfected the electronic flash in photography and pioneered the field of stroboscopy. In 1913, when he was ten, he was already playing with the power of light, constructing a powerful lamp for the night sky out of a gallon-size tin can, an electric bulb, and a wooden post. To optimize the effect, he climbed up on the roof of his Nebraska home and shone the light on the heavens with utter success, right up until the moment his parents found out. After that, he was instructed to stay off the roof and devise safer ways to see new things, which he did.

Only a few years earlier, a sixteen-year-old boy in Columbus, Ohio, had also taken to the sky, with a plan to ascend much higher than the

Edgertons' roofline. Cromwell Dixon labored night and day over the invention of the Sky Bicycle. Growing up just before the airplane was introduced, he was fascinated with flight in lighter-than-air craft. At the time, motorized dirigibles, introduced by Alberto Santos-Dumont, were regarded as the future of flight. Dixon, gazing at the clouds from his backyard in Columbus, wondered why that future couldn't also encompass personal, non-motorized transportation. No one else in the Dixon family knew much about invention, but somehow young Cromwell did. "From almost babyhood up," as a family friend said, he had "shown an inventive precocity." Entering his teens, he built a camera of his own design, along with a motor-driven roller coaster for the backyard. His mother, a widow who was independently wealthy, encouraged all of her son's enthusiasms. She even trusted him at the age of thirteen when he announced plans for the Sky Bicycle, a design that consisted of his own bicycle (without the wheels), suspended from a thirty-two-foot dirigible. Through pedal power, the pilot would control a set of propellers. Mrs. Dixon not only let Cromwell leave school to work on his invention, she poured thousands of dollars into it, specifying the finest Japanese silk for the balloon. She also insisted on sewing every stitch of the balloon, on which her son's life would depend. "Keep it up boy," he recalled her saying. "I know you are on the right track."

He was. The Sky Bicycle was a success from its first test flight, taking Cromwell Dixon up, where he wanted to be, and then allowing him to turn and swoop, just like a bird—a slow bird, admittedly.

At sixteen, Dixon was touring both the United States and Europe to demonstrate his Sky Bicycle, which he named the *Moon*. He was regarded as one of the premier "aeronauts" in the world, mentioned in company with Santos-Dumont and Captain Tom Baldwin. *Technical World* magazine analyzed the *Moon*, praising its "simplicity of construction" and clever design, but haughtily dismissing it as a toy that could never be used on windy days. The era of heavier-than-air craft, in other words, had arrived. Balloonists were out of style. In calm weather, though, the Sky Bicycle was safe and surprisingly easy to use. It made

Alberto Santos-Dumont.

Thomas Baldwin in his *California Arrow*.

Dixon a celebrity of the airshow circuit, where he invariably credited his mother as his inspiration. Mrs. Cromwell, though, was less happy with his decision a few years later to forsake his own invention for the heavier-than-air and faster-than-a-bicycle airplane.

In July 1911, Dixon, only nineteen, received his flying license, becoming the youngest recognized pilot in the country. He immediately accepted a job flying for the Glenn Curtiss airplane factory. It was a fantasy without equal in the first full blossom of the aviation era. And Dixon was a perfect symbol of that era, a young man born to fly. On the last day of September, two months after receiving a license, he made a mark as the first person to fly over the Continental Divide, the Rocky Mountains at their highest. He won a $10,000 prize for the feat. The next day, on a routine flight, a gust of wind sent his plane into the ground and he died a few hours later. Even at the end, Dixon was said to be courageous, trying to gain control of the plane as it swooped past a crowd of spectators; he was not screaming in horror, but merely shouting, "Here we go, here we go!"

Glenn L. Curtiss

• • •

Cromwell Dixon's whole life was the stuff of daydreams for any other kid—up to its early end. In his earlier incarnation, as the creator of the Sky Bicycle, he could have been a character in one the many children's books that made heroes of young innovators: the Motor Rangers, the Radio Boys, or, on the female side, the Outdoor Girls. The very closest fictional equivalent, though, was Tom Swift, star of *Tom Swift and His Sky Racer*, *Tom Swift and His Photo Telephone*, and *Tom Swift and His Electric Rifle*. In the books, launched in 1910, Tom was introduced as the son of an inventor. While the father was a relic of the nineteenth century, having given the world an improved butter churn, the son was a futurist, using his own abilities in combination with coming technology to escape danger. It was a twentieth-century point of view: to invent oneself out of trouble.

The Tom Swift series, which continues to this day, was not the inspiration of the author. In fact, the author didn't exist. The byline, "Victor Appleton," was as much a fiction as was Swift himself. Significantly, the series was conjured up by a literary agency, the Stratemeyer Syndicate, and it was specifically designed to sell books to boys by catering to their natural interest in inventing. That is not to say that girls did not have the same natural inclination, but they were already buying books in droves. Tom Swift was aimed at boys, and the series influenced generations of them. The publishers openly revealed their calculation on the early dust jackets: "Every boy possesses some form of inventive genius. Tom Swift is a bright, ingenious boy and his inventions and adventures make the most interesting kind of reading." Such comments were baldly aimed at parents who were hoping to bolster the inventive spirit in their own children. "It is the purpose of these spirited tales," explained another dust jacket blurb, "to convey in a realistic way the wonderful advances in land and sea locomotion and to interest the boy of the present in the hope that he may be a factor in aiding the marvelous development that is coming in the future."

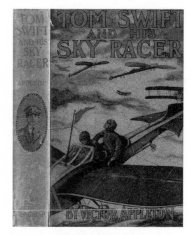

Cover of a Tom Swift book. The series continues to this day.

Alfred C. Gilbert, a graduate of Yale.

Two years after Tom Swift made his debut, Alfred C. Gilbert contrived to address the same yearning on the part of children: to invent. He introduced the Erector Set, a construction toy that offered miniature metal girders, nuts, and bolts. It was well received, but its fuller potential as an inventor's medium was unleashed when a small motor was included in the deluxe sets, allowing children to make their creations move and do work. The Erector Set was soon followed by other technology kits, presenting the basic tools of chemistry, radio, sound recording, and hydraulic engineering, among many others. In the early 1950s, the A. C. Gilbert Company introduced the U-238 Atomic Energy Lab, which came complete with a cloud chamber, an electroscope, nuclear spheres, and uranium-bearing ore. The Columbia University Physics Department ordered five of them. It sold very well, but it was withdrawn from the market when parents and others blanched, thinking about just exactly what a young person might invent with the U-238.

Gilbert, an Oregonian, was a graduate of Yale University. He opened his toy factory in New Haven and remained in close contact there with his alma mater. So it was that he heard in the late 1920s that the quiet old Chemistry Department was suddenly overwhelmed by students. The only explanation seemed to be that they had become interested in the subject as children by playing with chemistry sets made by Gilbert or another company, such as Chem-Craft of Hagerstown, Maryland. A chemistry professor at another college took a survey and reported that 70 percent of the students in his department had played with such chemistry sets when they were younger. For a toy, a chemistry set could have a lasting effect. "I thought you might be interested in knowing what happened to one of the kids who 'cut his teeth' on a Gilbert Chemistry Set," wrote a former customer to Gilbert, "so I am enclosing a reprint of a paper titled 'Determination of Oxygen in Titanium,' which I presented at the American Chemical Society." The other career sets were no less influential.

Some of the Gilbert sets came with plans for certain projects or activities. In 1941, the company even made a showcase of such ideas, opening the Gilbert Hall of Science on the corner of Fifth Avenue and Twenty-fifth Street in New York City: five stories of demonstrations and dioramas intended to inspire visitors with the breadth of possibilities open to owners of the various career sets. The emphasis, however, was on creativity, on children inventing their own toys, or on products of even wider interest: on the way out of the Hall of Science, young people were prodded by a list of items for which there was already a yearning. During the opening year, the imperatives included "a device to perfect the conversion of sound directly into printed form; an adhesive to make

An Erector Set owner's manual.

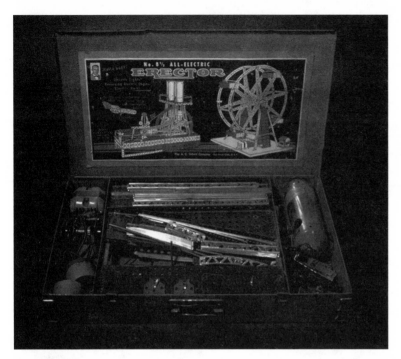

An Erector Set.

cellophane adhere to paper; material to which ice will not cling on airplane wings, highway surfaces, and windshields; lighter-weight batteries for portable radios; a cast iron that will bend; a substitute for paraffin; and an economical air conditioner for the automobile." The needs on the list were as neatly cut and packaged as one of Gilbert's sets. They certainly gave young inventors something to ponder, and in time, a variety of individuals would strike at least a few of the elusive inventions off the list.

Alfred C. Gilbert was an athlete at heart, a compact man who never seemed quite comfortable as an adult, having left behind his halcyon days of competition and triumph, especially in track and field. (At the 1908 Olympic Games, he was co-recipient of the gold medal in the pole vault.) He often referred to himself as a boy who never grew up. In that sense, he was ahead of his time. When he was growing up, adulthood was clearly delineated and generally taken quite seriously; by the time he died in the 1960s, adults were no longer expected to put away their toys and their enthusiasms, a trend that has grown more prevalent ever since. Toys now spark the imagination, or at least indulge it, across the generations.

Gilbert Hall of Science on the corner of Fifth Avenue and Twenty-fifth Street in New York City.

Gilbert often boasted of his understanding of American boys, and it can't be denied that he made a positive mark in millions of lives on that basis. In the process, however, he aimed his erector set and the other creative toys strictly at male children. "Hello, Boys," he would write in his many ads and newsletters, introducing his chatty sales text. While he may have succeeded in creating a certain clubby atmosphere around his educational toys, he failed to encompass the other half of his market: female children. It was probably bad business and it was certainly bad sociology. Led by the likes of Gilbert and the Stratemeyer Syndicate with its Tom Swift series, several generations of young women were tacitly discouraged from cultivating their basic instinct for inventing. Not that it stopped all of them, by any means, but the specter was there.

Lincoln Logs didn't make the same mistake. The company was founded in Chicago by John Lloyd Wright. His parents, Frank Lloyd Wright and Catherine Wright, were among the many progressives in the early 1900s who looked past stereotypes, filling the lives of their four sons and two daughters alike with creative toys. Wright, who would follow in his father's footsteps as an architect, invented Lincoln Logs in 1916. The interlocking wooden blocks were not the first cabin-building set, nor were they even the best. They were, however, marketed brilliantly, starting with the evocative name and the barrel packaging. Moreover, on the label, Lincoln Logs always showed both girls and boys building cabins. Advertising specifically cited the fun that girls could have, building structures to use with their other toys. The equal treatment was unarguably progressive. It also doubled sales. Wright's advanced thinking may well have helped Lincoln Logs survive the shifting market that eventually put the A. C. Gilbert Company out of business. The company did have lingering problems, though, in that no matter what a child created in a flight of brilliant imagination, it looked like a log cabin. The home office encouraged machine-age thinking by featuring photographs on the boxes of miniature gas stations constructed solely of the redwood blocks, but of course, they still looked like log cabins. And so did the automobiles.

At the 1908 Olympics, Alfred C. Gilbert was corecipient, with Edward Cook, of the gold medal in the pole vault.

The idea for Lincoln Logs struck John Lloyd Wright as he watched workers build one of his father's designs—an earthquake-proof building.

Lego's interlocking blocks have survived even more robustly as a medium for ideas or three-dimensional doodling. Introduced in 1932 in Denmark, Lego has remained loyal to its multicolored bricks, but in 1998, it jumped into robotics, offering sets that came with a list of accoutrements that amounted to an updated version of Gilbert's coveted electric motor: a microprocessor, lithium battery, servo motors, and an array of sensors including light, sound, touch, and ultrasonic. The company offends purists by offering plans for particular robots of its own design, but it also sponsors competitions for school-age innovators; fifty thousand entered into the program in the United States in 2005.

The world itself is toy enough for many children when it comes to inspiring invention. Everything that there is, after all, can be improved. A girl named Idaleen Root was nine when she noticed her mother having problems taking hot pies out of the oven. Whenever Mrs. Root used a thick potholder, she risked crushing the crust around the rim; when she used a thinner cloth, though, she was liable to burn her fingers. Idaleen invented a removable handle for her mother and later patented it.

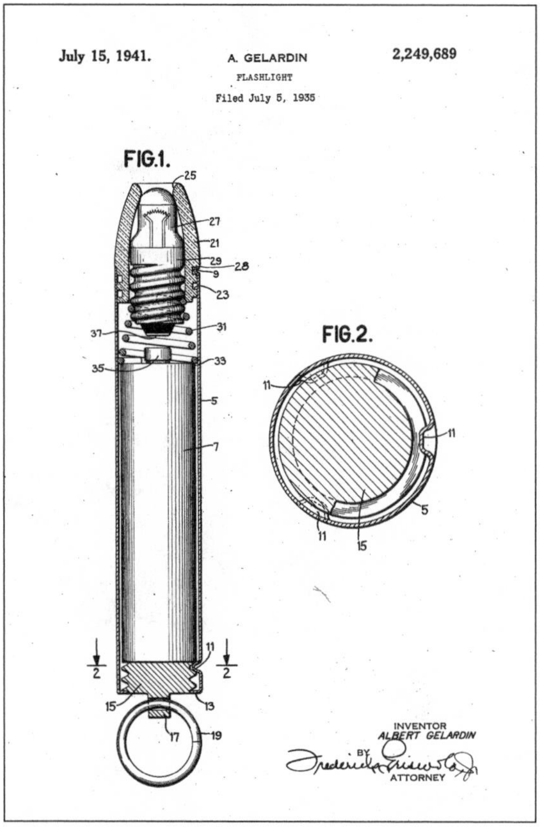

Albert Gelardin was just eight years old when he bought a diary and labeled it "My Inventions," recording within it the most fleeting of thoughts and the fullest of his plans. He kept up the diary all through his life, eventually making a living through successful variations on the pocket flashlight and the makeup compact.

John Jay Osborn, a freshman at Princeton University had always wanted an organ, and he indulged himself with a used one at a cost of $8. He practiced doggedly, his hands springing around the keyboard long after his legs grew tired of pumping the pedals that kept air in the pipes. In a flash, Osborn decided to automate the instrument. He knew just what to do: connect a vacuum cleaner to the air duct. It

July 15, 1941.   A. GELARDIN   2,249,689
FLASHLIGHT
Filed July 5, 1935

FIG.1.

FIG.2.

INVENTOR
ALBERT GELARDIN
BY
ATTORNEY

U.S. patent 2,249,689 for Albert Gelardin's flashlight, 1941.

worked brilliantly, in terms of Osborn's exhausted limbs. In terms of music, he couldn't be sure; it was hard to hear anything over the sound of the vacuum.

Frank Epperson, son of an office worker and a housewife in Oakland, California, woke up to his invention in 1905, a day after he mixed his own soda from a powdered mixture. Being eleven and having other things on his mind, he didn't measure it very carefully, and it turned out to be a rather flat, overly sweet soda. That is probably why he left it on the back porch with the spoon sticking out of the glass and thereupon forgot about it entirely. After a wintry night, he went out to the porch in the morning and noticed that his soda had hardened into a solid. Pulling it out of the glass by the handle of the spoon, he discovered that it was a likeably lickable confection.

Epperson didn't set out to invent anything, but he knew a good idea when it arrived at his door, even his back door, and he worked on refining the process, using test tubes as molds and small tongue depressors as handles. The following summer, he sold his modified icicles as "Epsicles" in Oakland's Idora Park. Had his family known anything about business or patent law, he might have been a prodigy at twelve. Instead, his invention remained in the neighborhood until he left for service as an aviator in World War I. When the war was over, he returned to Oakland and the Epsicle, renaming it the Popsicle and applying for a patent in 1924. Epperson never made much money on it though, selling the last of his rights during the Depression. He became a real estate developer but never stopped thinking of himself as an inventor. In his sixties, he developed a system of simplified spelling for the English language. "If it goes over," wrote an Oakland reporter in 1959, "it could do a lot more than the popsicle to make people happy."

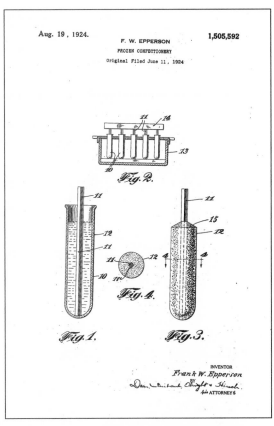

U.S. patent 1,505,592 for Frank Epperson's frozen popsicle, 1924.

• • •

In fortunate cases, children remain unjaded by the worldly wisdom of what is possible and impossible. With that brash confidence attractive in the young or inventive, or both, school-age innovators have intrepidly pursued the steepest of challenges, problems that stalled the best efforts of whole teams of their elder engineers and scientists. When Joseph Francis was a boy along the Massachusetts coast, shipwrecks were typically fatal for everyone onboard, even when land was in sight. Francis didn't think it had to be that way.

The long legacy of unnecessary tragedy upset Francis. At the time, the usual method for rescue was to send another boat, which was to be attached, if possible, to the sinking one by a long cable known as a hawser. People had to climb across the hawser, which was daunting, if not suicidal, in pitching seas. Worse, the rescue boat sometimes collided with the wreck and was itself lost. As it had been thus for centuries, no one was looking for an answer because the question was not being posed by anyone but little Joseph Francis: could a specially designed rescue boat save more lives? In 1825, at the age of eleven, he invented something entirely new and gave it a name never heard before: the lifeboat.

Francis took an old rowboat and built compartments in the bow and stern, filling each of them with cork. To his delight, the boat proved to be unsinkable, even with four grown men inside trying to tip it over. Francis won a prize at the Massachusetts Mechanics Institute for the design and, as an early report put it, "men of brains and money became interested in him." Francis' boat was first adopted by royal families as an unsinkable launch for short trips. More slowly, it inspired the establishment of rescue squads along coastlines around the world. Such efforts accelerated after Francis invented an iron-hulled version of his boat, a craft that could withstand the battering of a typical rescue. He followed it with a "lifecar," a fully enclosed vessel that actually ran along the hawser. Joseph Francis died in 1893, just as ships were themselves beginning to be equipped with lifeboats. He had received a lapelful of

Thaddeus Lowe's airship *The City of New York* with flags flying and the thirty-foot Joseph Francis lifeboat underneath.

Marion O'Brien Donovan

Early in 1941, Marion O'Brien was described by a potential employer as "attractive, about twenty-two years of age, with a good sense of humor and lots of ideas." A snappy dresser, O'Brien was looking for work with a fashion magazine, but in her spare time, she couldn't help inventing. It was a habit she came by naturally.

O'Brien's father, Miles, had worked briefly for Thomas Edison, who recognized the young Miles' raw ambition and suggested that he enroll in an engineering course. Miles hastened to act on the advice, entering Purdue University in company with his twin brother, John. They stayed in Indiana afterward and founded the South Bend Lathe Works, which would become not only the nation's largest exclusive manufacturer of lathes but also Marion O'Brien's personal playground as she was growing up. After college and a tour of Europe, Marion moved to New York, seeking the big time. She found it, but not in fashion magazines.

Even as she put in time at *Vogue* and *Harper's Bazaar*, she was in the process of patenting her first invention, a bracelet with a practical turn, holding keys, rather than charms, for ornamentation. More followed, and O'Brien became a prosperous inventor. Along the way she married a man named Donovan and became a mother. That didn't mean she stopped inventing. With babies in the house, she couldn't help but notice that diaper technology was woefully inadequate from the point of view of both mother and child—but mostly the mother. When a diaper was wet, for example, so was anything touching it, such as a sofa, a bedspread, or an evening gown. One day in 1949, Marion Donovan invented the moisture-proof liner for diapers, cutting up a shower curtain for the prototype. She promptly

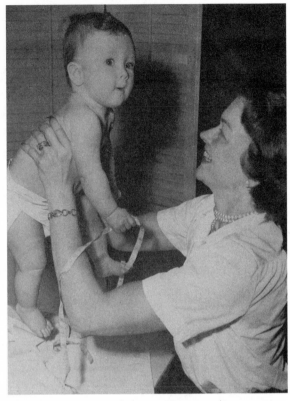

Marion O'Brien Donovan with one of the beneficiaries of her diaper research.

sold the patent rights for a handsome sum. Two years later, she patented the disposable diaper (which was subsequently refined by Proctor & Gamble chemist Victor Mills). "Though I have had no practical courses in design," Donovan once wrote, "I have studied it considerably on my own initiative." Donovan would continue inventing all of her life, with initiative supported by a firsthand understanding of manufacturing—and "lots of ideas."

awards and medals through the years, from governments grateful for the seventy-year commitment he had shown to an idea he'd had when he was eleven.

Ernest Patrick of Columbus, Indiana, was a high school dropout in 1932 when he built a radio that operated without tubes (those glass-encased converters that were the basis of early electronics). At the time, the tubeless radio was regarded as one of the most urgent inventions yet to be realized. Vacuum tubes, which amplified the sound, depended on heat to release electrons from the filament. They used a great deal of electricity simply to heat the filament. Aside from that, they were cumbersome and fragile. Patrick, in his late teens, stepped up with a solution.

Patrick was a typical small-town boy, though descriptions in the national press made him sound as though he were an exhibit at a natural history museum: the "mountain boy inventor," they called him. The inside of Patrick's radio was not filled with the usual double line of glass tubes. Instead, it contained "a bewildering jamble of copper wire." To some extent it worked, and the mountain boy inventor was taken very seriously. A group of businessmen from Chicago invested in his idea and engaged a British physicist to serve as his advisor. Moreover, the Institute of Radio Engineers, an august technical society, expressed interest in the invention. After six years of work, though, Patrick couldn't quite answer the society's sole requirement: that the tubeless radio surpass radios equipped with vacuum tubes.

Patrick was in the same position as another inventor in his late teens, a boy from Georgia who made a preliminary demonstration of his idea for using bismuth, a brittle element, in place of the tubes. He seemed to be close to a breakthrough, and a research organization offered him $3 million for the fully developed invention. As a general rule, an invention coalesces en route from its first stage as a crude but workable idea to its next as a promising reality. The most demanding stage is the last 2 percent's worth of refinement, by which the invention is made to work, not just sometimes, but all the time, under all possible conditions. Just that close to renown, the young Georgian couldn't close the last gap. Fate would have been kinder to ignore him in the first place.

An Idaho farm boy was yet another unlikely figure to rise to the center of attention in the field of electronic technology. "While great electrical engineers of the east are experimenting in their own way toward the perfection of television," ran a 1928 report, a "youth of twenty-two comes forth with an entirely different scheme. The youngster is Philo T. Farnsworth."

The columnist Drew Pearson once divided child inventors into two categories: those who had a patent attorney for a parent and those who didn't. Not that a child born into the business, so to speak, couldn't have a brilliant sense of invention, but suspicions naturally arise that the motivation belongs largely to the parent, while the child goes along for the ride. That was not the case with Philo Farnsworth. His parents were tenant farmers in Utah and Idaho, moving every few years in search of better land. They couldn't afford an automobile, so even in the motor age

A young Philo T. Farnsworth.

of the 1920s, they depended on horse-drawn wagons. Philo was something of a prodigy in mathematics and science, but overall he was an average student who was expected to work long hours on the farm before and after school. For all of his rustic surroundings, however, he did have advantages.

In the first place, Farnsworth had a father who consistently found time to take him by wagon to the nearest library—even though it might be half a day away. Mr. Farnsworth believed in his son and was even willing to turn the tables and play the role of assistant whenever Philo needed help with experiments. Philo's mother was torn when it came to his appetite for invention. She fretted that his reading in science took away from his violin practice. Yet she delighted in the automatic clothes-washing machine that he constructed for her.

In 1921, when young Farnsworth was sixteen, few people in his neighborhood knew anything about radio, broadcasting not yet having taken hold in many places, let alone rural Idaho. Farnsworth, however, was already working on television. In well-funded laboratories in Great Britain and the United States, television was being developed on a system of discs, spinning rapidly across an image in order to send and receive it. The discs, however, had drawbacks that had stymied the research community. For example, the discs at either end of the system had to be precisely coordinated or the picture would be blurry. In addition, the process was cumbersome, at its best in showing still pictures, or very slow-moving people.

While the "great electrical engineers of the east" were busy synchronizing their discs, Farnsworth was walking behind a plow, doing his chores on the farm. His head was filled with television though—making him the first of a long line of teenagers of whom that could be said. He had already considered the advantage of using a photoelectric cell to absorb the image electrically. As he later recalled, the straight lines of the furrows across the field then suggested an entirely new approach to the problem of transmitting the result: scanning a scene with a moving electron beam to create a pattern of horizontal lines (like the ones in the farm field).

Nipkow disc.

Farnsworth was in such a reverie that he failed to realize that his three-horse plow team was out of control and wandering near a ditch. When his father, Lewis, came upon the scene, the horses were in danger of harming themselves—and Philo. Lewis Farnsworth carefully took the horses in hand and then turned to discipline his son. Philo, however, had already started on an excited description of his new theory on television. By the time he was through, the elder Farnsworth couldn't even try to be angry.

Farnsworth explained the idea to his science teacher, who did not give in to the easy temptation to reject it simply because it came from a kid in an Idaho farm town and not from an institute, a professor, or a major corporation. He told Farnsworth to pursue it: "Study like the devil," he advised, "and keep mum."

The limitations of rural Idaho eventually hobbled Philo's efforts to equip himself for a career in electronics and invention. Therefore, Lewis made the decision to move his family to Provo, Utah, a college town where educational opportunities were a better match for the aptitudes of his children, Philo in particular. To earn money, Lewis Farnsworth traveled to construction jobs around the state.

Electrical engineering was simple for Farnsworth. What baffled him, and most other in-

Philo T. Farnsworth with his television camera, 1934.

ventors, was the rest of the world—any part that was larger than an electron. As a teenager, Farnsworth invented a radio dial that improved the accuracy of the tuning. A patent seemed to be in order, but applying for it required money. His father stepped in with hard-earned savings, set aside in those few years when there wasn't either a drought or a market glut in the agricultural business along the Utah-Idaho border. Philo found a lawyer through an advertisement in a science magazine, and Mr. Farnsworth sent him the $200 fee. That was the last they heard of the lawyer or their money. It was a low point, but it didn't stop either of them: Philo or the father who couldn't understand his boy's ideas but believed in them anyway.

 **CHAPTER THREE**

The Gathering of Minds

JOURNALS, FAIRS, AND UNIVERSITIES

*I*n 1844, the number of patents issued by the U.S. government totaled all of 507. Just fifty years later, the figure had grown to 19,146. The simplest explanations for the increase lay with far-reaching trends, such as the nation's population growth and the embrace of industrialization. Less obvious and yet just as important was the influence of a single trade magazine.

Scientific American magazine offered the first means by which inventors in America could peek over the fence to see the rest of the inventing community and find their bearings within it. An inventor who is in the position of working all alone nonetheless needs company: personalities and currents that circle close enough to enlighten but not so near as to constict. Up until the 1840s, the stubborn independence of the Yankee tinkerer wasn't just picturesque; it was well enforced by the difficulty of learning just who was doing what in any field of technology.

When *Scientific American* was launched in 1845, it was the only magazine of its type, a journal of practical science, specifically designed, as announced in its own columns, "to encourage and excite a spirit of enterprise and ambition in artists, manufacturers, and mechanics." The magazine was a success from the start, locating hundreds of thousands of people fascinated by invention and giving them a newborn sense of cohesion: a whole world of innovation existed within the universe of American life. *Scientific American* discovered it first and was its chronicle. Eventually, foreign-language editions embraced the same culture of invention in Europe and Asia.

The early issues answered technical questions, such as that from a person who asked how wide the opening in his sawmill would have to be to allow for a certain quantity of water. The figure was supplied by the editors, along with a formula, which they boasted was "never before published," for calculating the velocity of water coming through a hole. The technical education offered in the issues was sporadic, but it underscored the seriousness of the undertaking at hand. To leaven the hard facts of physics, *Scientific American* offered a large store of jokes, even ones about sawmills:

Scientific American magazine, launched in 1845.

A man in Orange county was found one night climbing an over-shot wheel in a fulling mill. He was asked what he was doing. He said he was "trying to go up to bed, but some how or other these stairs won't hold still."

Any community needs its own jokes, after all. And also a dose of medicine: the editors couldn't resist warning that many people try to climb "fortune's ladder" on the same principle used by the fellow in the fuller's mill. More optimistically, they published news on the introduction of a constant stream of new inventions, from cheese presses to color printing presses, windlasses to fire engines. Some received only the barest of notices, but the most intriguing were depicted in clear line drawings. An overall sense of encouragement came through on every page, but especially in the unrestrained coverage of change wrought by inventions throughout society. The tone, in one issue after another, promoted the belief that time itself could be judged on an inventors' scale—not as before by the lives of kings or the dates on the calendar, but by the technology unfolding along its own newly created continuum.

Scientific American, which was itself born almost simultaneously with the installation of commercial telegraph lines, published any and all news of the expansion of the wires. Its account of the opening of the 507-mile line from New York to Buffalo reads like a play, as Samuel Morse himself operated the key in New York, along with his friend, the politician Fernando Wood:

Telegraph lines, 1856.

"The compliments of the ALBANY Office to Prof. Morse and Mr. Wood."

"Utica Office wishes to be remembered to Prof. Morse and Mr. Wood."

"Auburn Office sends compliments to Prof. Morse and Mr. Wood."

"Buffalo sends compliments to Prof. Morse and Mr. Wood, and presents Lake Erie to Old Ocean."

Daguerreotype of Samuel Morse.

"Rochester Office sends compliments to Prof. Morse and Mr. Wood, and presents Erie Canal to Croton Aqueduct."

"Auburn presents State Prison to the Tombs."

"Syracuse sends compliments to Prof. Morse, and asks how are the Yorkers."

"Troy says, Now give me a chance. Compliments to Prof. Morse and Mr. Wood; and now for business, if there is any."

"Utica asks, Need we keep dark any longer?"

"Troy answers, No. Announce it to the four winds that Buffalo and New York are no longer separated—they talk to each other by lightning."

For more than a century, *Scientific American* was the favorite reading of the amateur inventor, as well as those who made a living in the field. The magazine's offices were located in New York City. A visiting reporter described them in 1889 as an "extensive and elegantly equipped establishment, with its walnut counters, desks and chairs." Most successful magazines are quite the opposite: cramped for space and decorated in a style that leans closer to hectic than hardwood. The reason for *Scientific American*'s sense of elegance was that the company had become one part magazine and one part law firm.

Believing in its own sermon, *Scientific American* branched out as a patent agency, running advertisements in hundreds of local newspapers as it promised to shepherd customers through the patent process. By 1889, the firm calculated that it had submitted applications for more than 100,000 patents. Depending on how many were accepted (probably somewhat more than the overall average at the time of 66 percent), *Scientific American* accounted for approximately one-fifth of all the patents granted between 1845 and the end of the century. Through its editorial influence on inventors

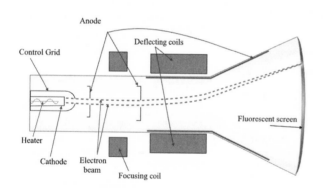

Diagram of a cathode ray tube.

from Thomas Edison to nuclear physicist Edward Teller, as well as through the solicitation business, which made the patent process accessible, *Scientific American* was a fundamental factor in building the culture of invention.

The original *Scientific American* spawned imitators, including *Science and Invention*. In one of the farmhouses that the Farnsworth family rented in rural Idaho, Philo found a pile of *Science and Invention* magazines left behind in the attic. He fell on them as though they were nourishment for a castaway, which, in a way, they were. In an issue published in about 1918, he read of the earliest experiments with television, by which discs were used to read images and transmit impulses representing light or dark. In another copy, he read about cathode ray tubes and the use of magnetic fields to direct their beams. In Farnsworth's recollection, that tattered pile of *Science and Invention* magazines, gathering cobwebs on the floor of the attic, contained two of the concepts crucial to the century's favorite invention. It only needed the right person to read them. Eventually, Farnsworth's concepts would prevail in the realization of television.

By the mid-twentieth century, *Scientific American* had lost its place as the epicenter of inventing. With technological fields burgeoning, readers were drawn to magazines reflecting more specific fields of interest. In trying to remain general in scope, *Scientific American* had become somewhat stodgy—and had long since stopped printing jokes about water wheels or anything else. It was replaced as the amateur's best friend by *Popular Mechanics*, a well-illustrated magazine founded in 1894 that was even more bold in cracking open the door to the future and giving a glimpse of what was inside. Its policy was to fill the first part of each issue with news of inventions, including predictions of barely imaginable advances yet to come, and the second part with plans for more familiar projects, from radio sets to backyard sheds. Both sections prodded something in the home tinkerer.

In between reports on metal wallpaper, automatic irons, and undroppable spoon holders, *Popular Mechanics* actively pursued anyone who might be qualified to write about upcoming epochs in human his-

Lewis Latimer (1848–1928) wrote *Incandescent Electric Lighting*, an important and influential book on electric lighting, in 1890. Born to fugitive slaves in Boston, Latimer started as an office assistant with a patent agency. He was soon an expert draftsman, and made patent drawings for Bell's telephone. Hiram Maxim, founder of the U.S. Electric Lighting Company, was impressed by Latimer's drafting skills and hired him in 1880 to do drawings for his company's patent applications. But Latimer was also a skilled inventor who designed several improvements for light bulbs during his time at U.S. Electric. Edison later asked him to write the book about the epochal invention "to meet," as Latimer wrote, "the want among the intelligent laity for a general knowledge of this subject," from the perspective of someone who had been part of its earliest years.

tory. In 1904, Jules Verne, the author of *Twenty Thousand Leagues Under the Sea*, was asked to discuss the future of submarines. First of all, he admitted that he wasn't actually much of an authority on submarines, that in his book he had taken advantage of his right as a fiction writer to make up anything he didn't know. But he tried and, as a resident of the tense continent of Europe circa 1904, he did predict that the future of the submarine was "to be wholly a war future." He argued against passenger liners beneath the water and was right, but, curiously, he failed to recognize the use of underwater vessels in scientific exploration of the type that his fictional *Nautilus* had undertaken.

In 1932, Sir Winston Churchill wrote a long article for *Popular Mechanics* on the future of the world and very specifically discussed a number of potential energy sources, including solar and nuclear power as well as hydrogen fusion. In a more general way, his words indicate that he wouldn't have been a bit surprised by the advent of the Internet, which arrived in common use about twenty-five years after his death in 1965. "Wireless telephones and television," Sir Winston wrote, "following naturally upon their present path of development, would enable their owner to connect up to any room similarly equipped and hear and take part in the conversation as well as if he put his head through the window. The congregation of men in cities would become superfluous. It would be rarely necessary to call in person on any but the most intimate friends. . . . The cities and the countryside would become indistinguishable." Even if he didn't describe every specific, he certainly recognized the effect it would have on society.

Popular Mechanics itself was less accurate in its own forecast of future technology, as it depicted life in the year 2000 as part of an article in a 1950 issue. Aside from disposable clothing, triple-decker highways even in small towns, and a synthetic living room that could be hosed down for easy cleaning, the magazine made the most frightening prediction in the long history of futurism. In the world of 2000, as the magazine described it, "discarded paper table 'linen' and rayon underwear are bought by chemical factories to be converted into candy."

Winston Churchill at a dinner party for the coronation of King George VI, 1937.

THE SPIRIT OF INVENTION

The intention of magazines such as *Popular Mechanics* and its herd of imitators was to encourage readers to look forward—and also, apparently, to give up candy. In older generations the tendency had been to look to tradition; the new impetus was to depend on change itself for comfort. Magazines played a disproportionate role in instigating that attitude and sparking the pursuit of invention to greater and faster levels. They are no less important in that regard today, though they are splintered into thousands of niches, appealing to inventors in particular fields. While *Popular Mechanics* forges on in much its usual style, *Scientific American* transformed itself into a magazine of studious perspective in the last part of the twentieth century. Its place as a forum for news on invention was taken by *Technology Review*, a publication of the Massachusetts Institute of Technology. A plethora of Web sites and even television programs also cater to the world of inventors, following the mission of the original *Scientific American* "to encourage and excite."

Cover of *Popular Mechanics*.

The beauty of magazines is that they can reach anywhere, to Idaho attics and Hawaiian islands, giving every reader the same information. The exposition, which is the three-dimensional version of the magazine in terms of generating the spirit of community, is as democratic, but it requires travel. The earliest fairs for exhibiting inventions in the United States were held at mechanics' halls in those cities fortunate enough to have one. They were highly suitable for distributing bragging rights in a particular locale. They were less successful in giving inventors the fullest possible sense of the latest developments across the whole field. In 1851, Great Britain brought forth an exposition that was equal to the task.

America and most other nations looked with awe and envy on the Great Exhibition of the Industry of All Nations, staged in London, the first of what came to be known as World's Fairs, with exhibits on the latest technology from around the world. The London fair was held in a magnificent structure made of iron and glass, the Crystal Palace, a name that attached to the fair as well. Two years later, organizers in the United States staged their own exhibition in a glass building in New York City that they also called the Crystal Palace. Fortunately, the exhibitors themselves were more original, bringing inventions that crammed the main building so full that it never did seem to be organized enough to open. It opened anyway, on July 14, 1853.

New York City went "Crystal" crazy in its wake, with doors opening nearby on the Crystal Stables, the Crystal Cake Shops, and Crystal Ice

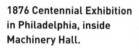
1876 Centennial Exhibition in Philadelphia, inside Machinery Hall.

Cream Saloons. A peddler woman even tacked a sign above her green-grocery kiosk and christened it the Crystal Fruit Stall.

People from all over the world were invited to send exhibits, and they did, but most of the foreign offerings were in the line of goods and artwork—such as vermouth from Italy and paintings from Holland. The Americans more than made up the difference in inventions, the volume and brash variety of their ideas constituting a kind of inventors' declaration of independence from Europe. Anyone who visited the New York version of the Crystal Palace could see at a glance that in terms of useful improvements to every phase of life, the New World was no longer looking to the Old.

For the participants, the New York Crystal Palace was a convention of all kinds of conventions. The candlemakers no doubt congregated after hours to trade gossip surrounding their display, a life-size wax sculpture of an ancient Greek slave with a wick in the top of her head. The machinists got together to debate the South's proudest display, a full-size steam locomotive that was as well engineered as it was gorgeous to behold. Having met one another in person on a national basis, the inventors were confronted with their own potential for the first time. Their shop talk led to the formation of the National Inventors Union, which seemed a natural idea, though it didn't last. Neither did any of the other attempts through the years to develop a tightly focused organization for those in the field. On the local or club level, hundreds of inventors' groups exist today, but an inventors' union apparently asks more than it can give, demanding loyalty of a band of born mavericks.

Through the years, other Grand Exhibitions seemed to arise just in time to mark new epochs in innovation. The 1876 Centennial Exhibition in Philadelphia was so rife with astounding inventions that visitors barely even noticed Alexander Graham Bell's demonstrations of

THE STRIDE OF A CENTURY.

A cartoon celebrating the centennial of the United States. The figure of Brother Jonathan, a precursor of Uncle Sam, straddles the towers of the main building at the Philadelphia World's Fair of 1876. Between his feet the North American continent, crossed by a railroad, appears on a half globe. Hot air balloons labeled "1776" and "1876" rise toward the top of the print on either side.

the telephone. At another booth, they could see a typewriter up close and for fifty cents have a letter typed to send to someone back home. Among the English exhibits were "some singularly homely road locomotives," according to a New York reporter. "These are seldom seen in this country, because of the inferiority of our roads; neither, indeed, are they very common in England, where much attention is being paid to the subject of steam transit over ordinary roadways." The exhibits may have been homely, but they set some Americans thinking about the possibility of automobiles.

Two of the most exciting displays promised energy—which strikes many an inventor the way a blank canvas inspires an artist.

The French sent a pair of Gramme dynamos to Philadelphia. Invented by a Belgian, Zénobe Gramme, seven years before, the dynamo is an efficient generator capable of converting mechanical power into electricity. The dynamos at the Centennial could produce a continuous output of voltage or, when they were properly arranged, act as an electric motor. That the Gramme embodied an estimable design is demonstrated by the fact that its inner workings of coils and armatures are still recognizable in modern direct-current generators. At the dawn of the electric age in 1876, the Gramme dynamo was a beacon that would attract thousands of other inventions.

The torch and part of the arm of the Statue of Liberty on display at the 1876 Centennial Exhibition in Philadelphia. There is an information booth at the base of the arm. Two persons stand behind the railing below the flame of the torch.

Alexander Graham Bell.

THE SPIRIT OF INVENTION

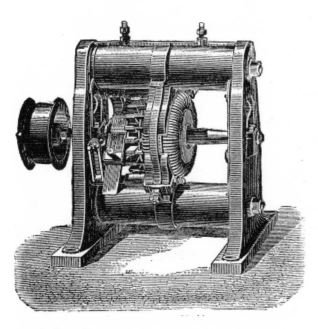
The Gramme dynamo.

Zénobe Gramme.

Machinery Hall covered thirteen acres and in all contained eight thousand machines for use in everything from candymaking to baby feeding. "It is in these things of iron and steel," said the writer William Dean Howells after gazing at the variety of inventions on display, "that the national genius most freely speaks." Nearly all of the hall's busy machines were powered by a single source: the magnificent Corliss engine, made in Rhode Island and regarded as the largest steam engine in the world. It delivered power through leather belts strung along the ceiling and dropping down to the various booths below. Visitors looked at the seventy-foot-tall Corliss engine as a wonder, expanding in many a mind's eye the potential of the factory floor. Where formerly a good-size plant had been measured in square feet, starting with the epoch opened by the first stroke of the Corliss engine at Philadelphia in 1876 it was measured in acres.

U.S. President Ulysses S. Grant and Brazilian Emperor Don Pedro starting the Corliss engine at the Philadelphia Centennial Exhibition.

The fountains and sculpture of the Court of Honor at the Chicago World's Columbian Exposition, 1893.

Chicago's Columbian Exposition of 1893, the Chicago World's Fair in 1933, the New York World's Fairs of 1939 and 1964: each was a defining showcase for invention. Perhaps the great fairs were indeed scheduled mainly to coincide with the enthusiasm and ready cash of the promoters, yet each in its own time greeted a new wave of curiosity about imminent change—and met it head-on. The 1939 fair introduced electronics. The 1964 edition gave people a glimpse of the computer age.

The great fairs petered out with the end of the twentieth century, being too general in scope to attract a generation used to traveling for trade shows and conventions concentrated on a particular subject.

The largest trade show in the United States has perennially been the Consumer Electronics Show, which covers forty-two acres and draws 140,000 people. It has witnessed the debut of dozens of recognizable inventions,

New York World's Fair of 1964.

An attendee at the 2008 International Consumer Electronics Show
watches a demonstration of the latest technology advances.

Video cassette recorder (VCR).

Compact disc (CD) player.

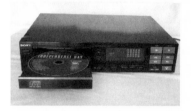
High-definition television (HDTV).

from the videocassette recorder (VCR) in 1970 to the compact disc (CD) player in 1981, the digital video disc (DVD) in 1996, and the high-definition television (HDTV) in 2003. Each was a major introduction, backed by the likes of Sony Corporation or Philips. At the International Housewares Show, another behemoth, the corporations make way for individual inventors, who are showcased in a special area, with their pistachio-nut openers or coffee-cup warmers.

As conduits for ideas, both magazines and fairs are themselves inventions, social machines that draw ideas through groups of people and spark ideas in the process. The process in each case is unregimented, if not haphazard, but then so are the natural environs of innovation. At roughly the same time they each developed to meet and simultaneously fuel the pace of invention, universities were emerging in new forms to take students on a slightly straighter line through an education in the art of inventing.

One of the earliest and most determined institutions was Purdue University in West Lafayette, Indiana. Founded in 1874 as a public land-grant college specializing in agricultural studies, it had a bit more cash than the average state school, owing to a generous gift from a businessman named John Purdue. In one of his rare speeches in 1876, Mr. Purdue proclaimed that he had searched the whole country for a suitable location for a college and found that "no place needed educational advantages worse that they did just here" in West Lafayette. In truth, the region did need higher educational opportunities— but first, it needed decent high schools. The initial wave of 126 applicants

Digital video disc (DVD).

THE SPIRIT OF INVENTION

to Purdue yielded only thirteen who were qualified for college studies. The more promising among the rest were relegated to a hastily organized preparatory school.

With certain voids at the start, such as students, Purdue endured a rocky beginning, with two presidents in the first two years of operation. The third president, Emerson White, stepped up to set a surprising goal for the young agricultural school, asserting that it would progress only after it was able to "provide instruction in the Applied Sciences, or Technology." The fields of applied science and industry, White felt, should be "close and fruitful, and the land-grant institution that falls short of this, fails to do what is most needed for the improvement not only of agriculture and the mechanical arts, but of all industrial interests and pursuits." In fact, no college in the country offered the type of course to which President White referred, whether it was called mechanical science or engineering. Even the Massachusetts Institute of Technology (MIT), organized in Boston in 1864, was still tilted toward the pure sciences, though it was said to be deeply influenced by a display at the Centennial Exhibition in Philadelphia showing the work of students at the Imperial Technical Institute of Moscow, a school with pursuits that were both scientific and staunchly practical. MIT would initiate its own mechanic arts course in 1876. As of that year, Purdue University was not exactly an obvious choice to join it at the forefront of college-level engineering. It had only one graduate. Nonetheless, it was about to have an electrical laboratory on a par with that of any university.

An early image of the Agricultural Engineering Building at Purdue University, founded in 1874.

Massachusetts Institute of Technology in Boston, organized in 1864.

John Purdue.

President White put his money—or John Purdue's money—where his mouth was, sending a professor named Harvey Wiley to the Centennial Exposition in Philadelphia. Wiley was given $1,000 and an order to bring back electrical equipment for Purdue. Some people spent a day at the fair. Professor Wiley devoted six weeks to it, with special attention to the exhibits in Mechanical Hall. All the while, he compiled his shopping list, blithely ignoring the fact that most of the students connected to Purdue were still struggling through courses in basic arithmetic and spelling.

"There were two dynamos on exhibition known as the Gramme Dynamo," recalled Wiley. "At the close of the exposition . . . the University of Pennsylvania bought the larger of the machines and I bought the smaller one for the young institution of learning, Purdue University." In November, after the Centennial Exposition was over, the dynamo was carefully packed and shipped to West Lafayette. A broad composition of cylindrical and circular casings, it stood about two-and-a-half feet high. For lack of a better location, it was installed in the chemistry lab. Confronted with the power promised by the dynamo, Professor Wiley was inspired to build an electric lamp, which he set up in the cupola on the roof of the building. He later boasted that he "illuminated the city of Lafayette late in November with the first electric light ever shown west of the Alleghenies and generated by a dynamo." So obviously ahead of its time, so surprisingly in the forefront of technology education, Purdue was imbued with a feeling of superiority over the preponderance of colleges, even the East's most prestigious ones, with their narrow dependence on classics and history. Purdue's early students felt that they were given something much more valuable to play with.

"Those of us who stood for Practical Mechanics," recalled William Goss, the Chemistry Department chairman, "entertained a belief that the education effects of the work which we were projecting was more significant than those which accrued from the training which characterized the old-time colleges. We were very likely mistaken in this assumption, but the zeal with which we promulgated it was an important factor in our success."

The zeal for the new type of schooling was contagious. The college's historian, H. B. Knoll, wrote of a graduate named David Edward Ross, "He did not distinguish himself as an undergraduate but in his senior year came under the influence of an early genius in radio, Reginald A. Fessenden, then professor of electrical engineering. Fessenden awoke him to the world of invention, helping to form a mind that afterward remained inquisitive and inquiring, ever searching for ways of better living." Ross invented a whole series of steering gears for automobiles but is best remembered for the thought he had on a walk late at night. Noticing that cats' eyes lit up when struck by the beams from automobile headlights, Ross went on to invent the reflectors that mark roads and traffic lanes. Ever humble in demeanor, he didn't name them after himself, but called them "cat's eyes."

Purdue developed courses in an array of engineering fields, as did an increasing number of universities at the beginning of the twentieth century. MIT was still at the forefront, along with the California Institute of Technology, formerly Throop College, in Pasadena. The revolution, however, extended to universities in all parts of the country and inevitably changed them from isolated islands of learning to capitals in the world of inventing.

At Purdue, Goss instituted a requirement that students actually make useful products. Deciding what to do with them was the problem for Purdue and other colleges through the years. In West Lafayette, Goss' department developed scores of innovations, including the educational Purdue lathe, which sold by the hundreds as industrial arts became standard electives in high schools around the country. Goss and his students also invented an early four-horsepower marine engine, conducting noisy tests on the Wabash River. It was a decided improvement over others on the market; in fact, the only thing wrong with it was that it was too apt to become a commercial success. Even while creating and building machines was considered a worthwhile endeavor at the school, entering the marketplace aggressively was considered a compromise in the goals of academia. Selling lathes to high schools was

Reginald A. Fessenden, an early authority on radio electronics at Purdue Univeristy and the mentor of David Ross.

Inventors' Contest

In 1929, Thomas Edison decided to give a full college scholarship to a deserving student, one who might even be described as his protégé and follow in his footsteps someday. The idea was a sensation in the national press. "Mr. Edison," suggested a writer for *Outlook* magazine, "is famous enough so that, if he wishes to choose a successor . . . by holding an all-American spelling bee, a jacks tournament or pancake-eating contest for that matter, no one will say him nay."

To choose the future Edison, the original Mr. Edison and his son, Charles, organized a kind of academic tournament, open to boys only, to which each state and the District of Columbia were to send an entrant. The boys would travel to Edison's lab in West Orange, New Jersey, where they would take a written test prepared by Edison and a few of his friends: Henry Ford, Harvey Firestone, Charles Lindbergh, George Eastman, and two educators, including the president of MIT. The first part of the test was composed of questions on physics, mathematics, and chemistry. One question, for example, was "Where in the universe would a body weigh nothing?" (Answer: nowhere, since even distant objects exert some attraction to each other.) Another part of the test posed questions of character or attitude, including "Describe an average day in your life when you are fifty years old." The third part required the entrants to write a generic letter requesting employment, and the fourth tested basic knowledge, along the lines of "Who was Jenny Lind?" and "What is a mammoth?" (a Swedish singer and a prehistoric mammal, decidedly in that order).

After pondering the question "If you were on a desert island without tools, how would you move a three-ton rock fifteen feet vertically and 100 feet horizontally?" Utah's entrant scrawled, "Why move a rock?" He didn't get the scholarship.

The winner was Wilber Huston of Seattle. He was an instant celebrity, labeled "America's Brightest Boy" and featured in a blanket of articles and on newsreels and radio shows. Huston chose to attend MIT, as did the 1930 winner, Arthur O. Williams of Providence, Rhode Island. With that, Edison announced that he would no longer sponsor scholarship contests. He was growing ill and died in October 1931.

Neither of the scholarship winners ultimately followed in Edison's footsteps in the field of invention, although both had careers in the sciences, Huston ending his career at NASA and Williams teaching physics at the college level. They were worthy enough recipients, but apparently it takes a test of more than four parts and questions of trivia to identify the inventing spirit.

consistent with the theme, but profiting from marine engines and other projects was regarded as an activity outside the purview of a dignified hall of learning. Little by little, that would change. The marine engine was never promoted beyond the Purdue campus.

Companies and industry groups peppered Purdue with engineering problems during the decades after World War I, sometimes providing funds for basic research, sometimes only the challenge of a good question. The Electrical Engineering Department, for example, worked with the telephone industry to develop a means of balancing the currents running through parallel telephone and power lines so that the charges carried wouldn't produce interference in the form of loud static on the phone line. For many years, the hallways in the department were strung with both kinds of lines as the professors and students looked for an alternative to copper wiring. They found an acceptable type of steel substitute just in time for the copper shortages of World War II.

More and more, universities became part of the inventing world, creating ambiguities between the high-minded goals of the school and the moneymaking potential of a good invention. In the years between the world wars, many universities joined a trend by authorizing research foundations. Nominally independent, foundations were charged with overseeing the funding of projects and holding patent rights on behalf of the associated university. The inventor or inventors typically received a portion of the net proceeds. Moreover, they were relieved of the tribulations of patent application. And for some inventors, that alone was reward enough. Among the schools to launch research foundations in the first wave of the 1920s were Cornell, Minnesota, Ohio State, Purdue, Virginia Polytechnic (Virginia Tech), Washington State, Wisconsin, and the University of Maine. Not coincidentally, all were state schools, in whole or in part. Government-sponsored schools had the stickiest situation where commercial activities were concerned. At the same time, private schools were trying to rise above the need for a special arrangement, relying instead on a gentleman's code by which campus inventors voluntarily turned over patent rights to the university. One by one, they found themselves snagged in fights over priority or remuneration, and one by one, they started research foundations; most universities today have some provision for the advent of invention in their midst.

In 1980, a new law called the Bayh-Dole Act encouraged universities to shed their traditionally passive role, that of waiting on the whims of industry. It provided that universities could actively promote inventions discovered under federal grants and pointedly granted incentives for universities to open "transfer offices" specifically to find uses and markets for campus inventions. In practice, the Bayh-Dole Act turned universities into invention shops, with ideas on the shelf and professionals to promote them in the marketplace. The shift did not please everyone. A pilot program on which the act was based, operated by the National Science Foundation at MIT, drew anger from Senator William Proxmire (D-Wisc.), who said that the patent rights to inventions developed in the project should go to "the government and taxpayers who paid for them . . . the National Science Foundation has no business in this personal profitmaking operation at M.I.T."

The Bayh-Dole Act succeeded in its two-pronged objective: to encourage universities to bring inventions out into the open and to provide a new revenue source for the schools. By the year 2000, every research university in the United States had a transfer office, and licensing revenues were increasing to the point that universities could sponsor their own research in marketable inventions, approaching industry not with the empty hands of a beggar but with a finished product available to the highest bidder. In just over one hundred years, universities had become powerful entities in the world of inventing. It was probably inevitable. Turning out inventors by the classful into a world hungry for their abilities, universities couldn't help but become agents of invention, not unlike journals and fairs, trafficking in the wares of the future.

CHAPTER FOUR

Mavericks at Work

THE INDUSTRIAL RESEARCH LABORATORY

*I*n the early 1880s, a metalworker from the state of Ohio heard that Thomas Edison had begun working on a way to purify iron-rich soil using electricity. With that, the Ohioan traveled to New Jersey, stepping off the train in Menlo Park, the tiny farm village that Edison had made world-famous. The visitor easily found Edison's white clapboard laboratory, by far the biggest building around, and wandered in. Stopping technicians to explain his interest in the experiments on iron, he was directed first to one department and then to another, but for the time being, no one seemed to know where Edison could be found.

Out on the street again, the Ohioan couldn't resist asking the locals about his hero. When the subject of one of Edison's many inventions

Thomas Edison.

Thomas Beddoes.

came up, a woman who lived in the vicinity interrupted. "He only got it accidentally," she announced.

Edison, however, was far too busy a man to await accidents. In fact, the primary goal of the laboratory at Menlo Park, opened in 1876, was the removal of chance from the equation of invention. In collecting experts in the physical sciences and giving them a place to work in a co-ordinated way, Edison unveiled his greatest creation of all, the one with the most far-reaching potential. As Matthew Josephson observed in his seminal biography, *Edison*, "No one had ever heard of a man setting up a center of research, a sort of 'scientific factory' in which investigation by a whole group or team would be organized and directed solely toward practical inventions."

Research institutes had existed in some measure before Menlo Park. Thomas Beddoes organized a very early example in Bristol,

Thomas Edison (*center, holding hat*) and his workers on the steps of the Menlo Park lab.

England, in 1800 to investigate the properties of gaseous elements, calling it the Pneumatic Institute. He was fortunate to sign Humphry Davy as one of its first investigators. Universities in the United States and elsewhere set aside laboratories for the use of faculty and students, but in all such cases the driving force was pure science: understanding the universe. Inventors are interested instead in applied science: taming the universe. For a long time, that was regarded as a solitary undertaking.

Thomas Edison's Menlo Park lab building.

Perhaps the hubris of daring to improve on life seemed necessarily to be harbored in a single human heart. On a more practical level, an untried idea by its very nature isn't easily communicated. For that reason, the only type of coordinated inventing known before Edison's time was found in the family setting, where the individual is commonly blurred into a group. A mother or father would hear out a new idea and invest in it. A sister or brother would share the work. A husband or wife would help to develop and escalate ideas. At the very least, they would all listen. On that basis, the most extensive development lab in the country, before Menlo Park, may well have been Herrick Aiken's front parlor in Franklin, New Hampshire.

The Aiken house brought together the talents of three active inventors: Herrick and his two sons. Herrick was a toolmaker who began to specialize in adapting European knitting equipment during the heyday of the New England

Humphry Davy.

textile industry in the mid-nineteenth century. Aiken's sons, Walter and Jonas, enthusiastically embraced their father's pursuits and delved not only into the engineering challenges attached to commercial knitting but into the social dilemmas as well. Among the three of them, the Aikens developed a series of industrial knitting machines in the 1850s, just in time to meet the demand for mass-produced clothing brought about by the mustering of troops in the Civil War. In fact, "among the three of them" may be the best way to place the credit for the family inventions.

In the process of installing Aiken Knitting Machines, Jonas Aiken, the younger of the sons, noticed that many people who worked as knitters in their homes were put out of work by the mechanized versions. And typically, women comprised the vast majority of home knitters—women who needed the livelihood that knitting provided. To give individuals a chance to compete with the factory-made knitwear, Jonas took it upon himself to develop a knitting machine for home use. He intended the machine, he later wrote, as "a blessing to the laboring poor." His goal was to make up for industrialization, or at least to reduce its disruptions, by giving knitting back to "a hundred thousand homes."

Jonas was supported by his father and brother, the latter accompanying him in 1858 to New York, where they displayed Aiken's Family Knitting Machine at the latest incarnation of the Crystal Palace exhibition. In 1860, Jonas wrote to his brother, who was to manufacture the invention, "I believe I cannot make the machine . . . more perfect than it is now." An inventor knows no finer feeling than is expressed by those words. To sell the new invention, Jonas built a national organization of distributorships, many of which he awarded to women, in keeping with one of his original goals for the machine. The success of the family knitter in the 1860s capped the fame of the Aikens as a family of inventors, their cartel of three minds being considered newsworthy at the time.

For the average inventor, finding as many as two other people to trust would be remarkable anywhere outside of the household. The fear of someone purloining a new idea has always encouraged inventors to keep to themselves, so Thomas Edison's rather sudden construction of a private research lab at Menlo Park was as much a revolution in human relations as it was a boon to the advancement of applied science.

Fresh off the invention of the quadruplex system of telegram transmission, Edison at the age of twenty-nine had a little money and all that he could stand for the time being of the brutality of business. He gave up his various operations elsewhere and invested his remaining capital in the new building in Menlo Park. The village, located in the northern part of New Jersey about twenty-five miles southwest of New York City, may as well have been in Siberia in 1876: a desolate and dispirited farm village, where a housing tract had recently been planned and then abandoned. Its appeal lay in the combination of quiet isolation and access to New York by a good train line. After the financing for the development

The research campus at Menlo Park, about twenty-five miles southwest of New York City.

Charles Steinmetz' Lightning Machine

When Charles Steinmetz was at college in his native Germany in the 1880s, he was exposed to an entirely new course of study: electrical engineering. He was irresistibly drawn to it, despite the fact that practically no one outside the field knew what it was. They could hardly be blamed. Electricity was hard to understand or even to see, except when a person happened to be looking in the right direction during a thunderstorm. Even then, when a lightning bolt hit, nature allowed only a fleeting glimpse.

Steinmetz moved to the United States as a young man, rising quickly in the growing community of electrical engineers in and around New York. When General Electric was organized, he found a permanent home in the city of Schenectady. Combining invention with pure scientific research, he held the title of consulting engineer, or in the words of a reporter from the *New York Times*, the unofficial title of "grand master" among electrical experts, of which GE had many.

One day in 1920, Steinmetz arrived at his summer camp along the Mohawk River to discover that a lightning bolt had ricocheted through the house, destroying some of the furniture. If the lightning had exerted any choice in the matter, it had picked on the wrong house and decidedly the wrong owner. Steinmetz took the whole episode as an affront, returning to his laboratory determined to manufacture his own lightning. Two years later he succeeded, making headlines as the first mortal with the power to throw lightning bolts. Steinmetz' invention consisted of a line of condensers that could be overcharged with two million volts of electric energy. As in the case of the clouds during a storm, the energy had to find its way to the earth, although in the GE laboratory, wires encouraged its path toward specific targets. Steinmetz had collected more than a hundred patents over the years, showing people the potential of electricity; he capped his career by showing them the actual article, at least for 1/100,000 of a second at a time.

fell through, Edison purchased open land at a bargain price and built the retreat that was described in 1880 as "a long, low, nondescript building that one might mistake for the barn of a New-Jersey farmer, only, as a rule, New-Jersey barns are very superior in their external appearance to Edison's laboratory." The bottom floor was devoted to offices and storage, while the laboratory occupied the upper floor. When the walls couldn't contain everything the researchers were thinking about inside, the laboratory spilled outside. Edison's thirty-five-acre tract soon included a grove of electric lampposts, neatly laid out in rows, and an electric train circling through the property at speeds of up to forty miles per hour.

Edison hadn't been in Menlo Park long when he was compelled to authorize funds for a picket fence. Cows kept wandering into the yard. As a matter of fact, security was less than tight throughout, as the metallurgist from Ohio had discovered. Anyone could stroll through. Those who did were free to watch Edison at work; unless he had reason to complain about visitors, he didn't mind their presence. Sometimes he didn't even notice it. At other times, he gave impromptu explanations of his work, the privilege being lost on many of the visitors, who didn't understand anything he was saying. In part, the mismatch lay in scientific principles and the jargon that expresses them. Yet there was another difference between the typical visitor on one hand, and Edison and his research team on the other. Edison was fundamentally a futurist, interpreting the coming age through his inventions the way archeologists interpret the past through artifacts. He was more comfortable thinking

Thomas Edison's electric train circling through the Menlo Park property.

five years or even just ten minutes into the future, when certain things would be different. Discerning what they would be—inventing them, in fact—was the role of the lab. His unfinished inventions were proof of the future, just as a Mayan vase is proof of the past. Most inventors favor Edison's outlook and it separates them from others, reinforcing the tradition of the lone inventor. At Menlo Park, however, the future engulfed them all under one roof.

An article in the *Telegraphic Journal* in 1878 recounted the visit of a reporter to the lab. "The front doors open directly into the office," he explained. As soon as the reporter entered, he noticed a man sitting at a table studying a mechanical drawing, and he asked him where to find Edison.

"Go right upstairs," said the employee casually, "and you'll find him singing into some instrument."

On that day Edison might have been working on refinements to the phonograph or the telephone. He liked to sing and did a lot of it to test each of them. On any given day, a person looking for him would do well to follow the sound of his voice. Edison might be found anywhere in the laboratory. He didn't have his own work area nor, by and large, did anyone else.

The lab itself reflected Edison's attitude. The research facility on the second floor of the building was a huge room, dotted with tables and freestanding equipment. The walls were lined with bottles and other supplies.

Thomas Edison and the phonograph, c. 1878.

Thomas Edison's carbon button transmitter for the mouthpiece of the telephone.

The ceiling was strung with wires. No warren of rooms hiding work from prying eyes, the lab was itself a work in progress, redesigning itself around the ideas that Edison and his men were pursuing. For assistance, Edison recruited about a dozen specialists in chemistry, glassblowing, or electricity, but the main body of the workforce of about twenty-five consisted of people who could and would do anything. William J. Hammer was one of them. On his first day, he approached Edison, who was operating a press, turning out cylinders made of chalk for use in the loudspeaking telephone. Hammer humbly asked Edison what he should do. Edison didn't pause. He didn't look up from the press. "Find something to do," he said.

William J. Hammer.

"In common with others," Hammer concluded, "I assisted in the general work going on." He took charge of operating and maintaining the vacuum pumps used in light bulb experiments, made calculations on the amount of copper wiring needed for the electrification of lower Manhattan, and kept the records on ongoing work with electric light. He was eventually credited with a role in promoting the first practical carbon-filament light bulb. Others had made substantive contributions as well, but it was Edison's name on the patents and, of course, his name that was attached to all of the wonders to emerge from Menlo Park, including the light bulb, power transmission, and improvements to the telephone and phonograph. Surprisingly few of his employees resented the way that, according to the system of Edison's "invention factory," as he called it, the boss received credit for their input as well as his. In a number of cases, former assistants left to work for themselves or the competition, but that problem was more pronounced among office employees than those in the laboratory. The Menlo Park crew, pursuing the goal of invention, needed Edison as director and coach more than he needed any of them individually, and so they were remarkably loyal. "Edison made your work interesting," recalled a worker named John Ott. "He made me feel that I was making something with him. I wasn't just a workman."

The lab at Menlo Park was a success from the start, producing many of Edison's most renowned inventions, from the power station to the electric railway—and some that were less heralded, such as the electric pen. The lab closed after only eight years, however, in part for personal reasons involving the founder's family. Edison's first wife, Mary, died at their home in Menlo Park in 1884 and Edison, in his grief, lost interest in the whole place. He went on to a larger laboratory in West Orange and other installations in New Jersey and Schenectady, New York. The building at Menlo Park fell into disuse and ultimately collapsed during a storm. The activity in the laboratory had, however, permanently changed attitudes toward invention.

With technology growing more complex in the late nineteenth century, a change may well have been inevitable. Much of human history

Thomas Edison's Menlo Park lab interior.

GE Schenectady works, c. 1886.

points toward a tendency to congregate for greater gain, of shipyards organizing to build a galleon rather than a skiff and then a battleship rather than a galleon. Edison demonstrated at Menlo Park that the same multiplier worked for pulling abstractions out of the air. Consumers delighted in the products pouring out of the lab at Menlo Park. Institutions, moreover, took note of the environment that produced them.

The General Electric Company, which was itself a by-product of Edison's Menlo Park researches, was the first corporation to formally establish a laboratory for advanced technology. The company had been founded out of a merger that included the Edison Machine Works in Schenectady, a small city that became the headquarters for the new concern. GE was entirely independent of Edison in 1900, when the chief engineer, Charles Steinmetz, convinced the officers to fund a research laboratory—one not unlike the one at Menlo Park. Ever since, the company has been fond of pointing out that the lab had its first home in a carriage barn behind Steinmetz' house.

As GE Research grew in stature and moved into a building meant for humans, it was pulled in three directions, a state of permanent identity crisis common to industrial research laboratories. With sharp scientists and unsurpassed equipment, the lab could refine existing products. It could invent new ones. Or it could experiment with technologies not yet harnessed to the extent of generating actual inventions.

Thomas Edison and Charles Steinmetz examining porcelain insulators that had been smashed by Steinmetz' artificial lightning, Schenectady, New York, 1922.

THE SPIRIT OF INVENTION

Steinmetz tried to inculcate his feeling that the lab should be an instrument of exploration not tied to quarterly statements. His colleague Willis R. Whitney, the first director of the lab, chimed in with his own justification for the laboratory, noting that it had only cost the company about $10,000 per year at the start. His point was that purchasing outside technology cost companies far more than the price of advanced research—and he was referring not only to dollars but also to loss of pride. Nonetheless, the research laboratory had to prove itself in more than interesting science. When the company was wrestling with a specific problem, its most astute researchers couldn't be aloof.

At the time, and for many years afterward, GE lived and died by the light bulb business—and in the early 1900s, its light bulbs were literally crumbling.

The light bulb as GE inherited it from Edison had a carbon filament as its source of illumination. It might have been a miracle in its time, but by the first years of the twentieth century, customers complained that it was too fragile. For the same reason, carbon filament bulbs couldn't be installed on trains or in any other jostling environment. In addition, they used a lot of electricity for the amount of light they emitted. Incandescent light bulbs might have been more efficient than whale oil or candle wax, but modern customers found them wanting nonetheless. The case of the delicate filament was a towering dilemma at GE, discussed in the executive offices, on the production floor, and throughout the research lab.

The lab, still in its infancy, made an attempt to invent an improvement. Willis Whitney tempered the carbon filament and produced a bulb that was better, but still not very good. In 1906, the company looked elsewhere. For an astounding $490,000, it purchased German patents covering a sturdier element for the filament: tungsten. The price was steep, but in the future that outlay would, ironically, benefit the research laboratory, fueling the argument that it was cheaper in the long run for the company to stay ahead of the industry than to catch up by paying for new advances.

Charles Steinmetz.

Irving Langmuir.

The sense of relief in the aftermath of the patent purchase was short-lived. The European breakthrough had its own set of problems, starting with the fact that tungsten was itself too fragile an element to withstand the manufacturing process necessary for making filaments. As of 1906, GE had piles of tungsten and a $490,000 patent, but the factories were still turning out light bulbs illuminated by a thread of carbon.

The research laboratory turned the problem over to a new recruit, thirty-two-year-old William Coolidge. A Massachusetts farm boy with the shy manner well suited to New Englanders, Coolidge had graduated from MIT and taken his doctorate in Germany. Returning to the United States, he worked for a time at MIT but was soon courted by Whitney. As C. Guy Suits, a later director of the lab, explained, "At that early period, persuading a university scientist that he might have a career in industrial research was not accomplished easily nor often." Coolidge, however, decided to give applied science a try. In the lab in Schenectady, he found all that any inventor could want: time, resources, and a difficult problem. Coolidge experimented with tungsten until he knew its every characteristic and expected its every quirk. After three years, he had perfected a process that induced the element into ultrathin wire at high temperatures.

Though William Coolidge received the credit for the widely heralded innovation, he was the first to insist that he had received help from the dozens of experts surrounding him. One of them was Irving Langmuir, a rather introverted scientist who had also been to graduate school in Germany and who had also chosen the GE Research Lab over a career in academia.

Langmuir boasted later in his career that he had never once embarked on research in search of a new product. For him the formula was reversed: invention emerged naturally from curiosity and knowledge. He and others at the lab were encouraged in that attitude by Whitney, who toured the workspace, asking in his witty, winning manner if everyone was having fun. With the right kind of employees, it was a valid question. Langmuir's particular fascination in 1910 revolved around changing the environment inside a vacuum chamber, such as a light bulb or, fittingly, a vacuum tube. He took Coolidge's light bulb as though it were a hand-off in football and ran with it. He filled the vacuum surrounding the tungsten with an argon/nitrogen gas that increased the efficiency of the bulb by 20 percent. Langmuir's work in optimizing the vacuum tube laid the basis for whole fields of consumer electronics, including the recording and radio industries. In keeping with his interest in molecular engineering, Langmuir also built upon Coolidge's advances by experimenting with electron emissions from charged tungsten in a vacuum atmosphere. He showed Coolidge and others in the lab how easily those emissions could be controlled. Coolidge took the ball back.

At the time, Will Coolidge's idea of "fun," and his most intense interest at the laboratory, lay with X-ray technology. The cold cathode tube had launched the field in the early 1890s, relying on aluminum in a gas-filled tube to emit the electrons that constituted X-rays. In 1913, Coolidge used a different construct, employing hot tungsten to elicit X-rays in an instrument under fairly high pressure. The resulting X-ray tube was more easily controlled and more durable than the previous one. It was readily accepted as a landmark in radiology.

Coolidge's experience over his first decade at GE proved Steinmetz' theory that knowledge about any slice of the physical universe served by the company would ultimately prove useful—and profitable. The trick in a research laboratory was to remain grounded in the world of applied science and yet to resist the temptation toward short-term thinking. Over the course of more than a hundred years, GE Research has at times been prey to the changing whims of management, which is, after all, paid for making the near future predictable. When Jack Welch was named CEO in 1981, he found ways to pressure the lab into concentrating closely on product development, all with an eye toward return on investment. It would have been hard to predict, however, that allowing William Coolidge to become a master of heated tungsten would eventually lead to the invention of the hot cathode tube, which is the basis of X-ray technology even today. A variation is also used in computerized

Mary Ann Strehlein

In 1968, a reporter from the *Chicago Tribune* paid a visit to Mary Ann Strehlein and riled the kindly inventor with the very first question. "I was told you are 81 years old," said the reporter, "and received a bachelor of philosophy degree from Northwestern University when you were 73. That's really something."

Strehlein interrupted, "They have that all wrong. That's not my age. I don't believe in age."

Strehlein had spent her career in the garment industry, dedicating her spare time to the perfection of the fastener, that bit of hardware that holds two pieces of cloth together. Along the way, she also found time to return to her academic career, long since interrupted, and graduated from Northwestern with the class of 1959.

The first of the seven patents issued to Strehlein between 1925 and 1967 covered an improvement on the hook and eye; the last of them described a far more sophisticated stud-and-latch combination that employed a spring. In times of strain on the fastener—as might develop after dessert was passed around for the second time—Strehlein's invention was designed to hold firm. "The more resistance, the tighter the fastener holds," she boasted. Her fastener was immediately placed on the market by an agency specializing in fasteners.

"I shall never retire," Strehlein insisted in her 1968 interview, when her age was indeed eighty-one. "I believe in activity."

"I have too much to do," she added.

axial tomography (CAT scan) machines, an important product for GE in the twenty-first century.

Coolidge, Langmuir, and their colleagues traded discoveries and invented side by side, sometimes in cooperation, sometimes in competition. The process reflected the basic strength of an institutional research lab.

While a research lab could never be quite as regimented as a factory floor, it also would never be as individual as a tinkerer's cottage. The industrial age had come to the process of invention. Willis Whitney, the director, tried to explain how the effect on inventing was even vaster than it looked. Fittingly, he relied on mathematical terms:

The mathematics of co-operation of men and tools is interesting in this connection. Separated men trying their individual experiments contribute in proportion to their numbers, and their work may be called mathematically additive. The effect of a single piece of apparatus given to one man is also additive only, but when a group of men are co-operating, as distinct from merely operating, their work rises with some higher power of the number than the first power. It approaches the square for two men and the cube for three. Two men co-operating with two different and special pieces of apparatus . . . are more powerful than their arithmetical sum. These facts doubtless assist as assets of a research laboratory.

One of the other positive aspects of a research lab is its natural ability to develop talent in young inventors.

In the late 1910s, Langmuir's work in the unique environment of the vacuum tube led him to renew his early interest in chemistry, and he designed ways to measure the presence and activity of atoms. His research eventually led to an even more narrowly focused interest in the manner by which certain solids absorb gases, which then form a top layer on the solid, changing or masking its properties. It was pioneering work, belonging to the realm of pure science, but Whitney encouraged Langmuir to continue. In 1918, Langmuir hired a new assistant to help him, a vivacious twenty-year-old named Katharine Burr Blodgett.

Blodgett was a native of Schenectady, her father having been a patent attorney for General Electric. Mr. Blodgett, however, died before Katharine was born, attacked in his home by a burglar. In the aftermath, Katharine's mother didn't cloister her children, as might be expected, but was dedicated to giving them a broad education, taking them to live in Europe, with occasional sojourns in New York to brush up their English. Katharine Blodgett took degrees at Bryn Mawr and the University of Chicago before applying for work at her father's old company, GE. In her work with Langmuir, she co-authored a number of scientific papers. Extending any credit at all to an underling was a generous gesture on Langmuir's part, yet even so he didn't believe that Blodgett could ever reach her potential by serving as his assistant. He encouraged her to apply to the doctoral program in physics at Cambridge University in England, the most advanced program in the world for her area of study.

British schools in the first half of the twentieth century were far less liberal than American ones in encouraging women to pursue degrees in math and the sciences. As a matter of fact, no female had ever been accepted at Cambridge for a doctorate in physics. Katharine Blodgett was anxious to try, however; her academic achievements qualified her, and Langmuir's recommendation overcame all less relevant objections. She was ultimately admitted and graduated in 1926, returning to Schenectady immediately afterward to work again under the aegis of Langmuir. In 1932, Langmuir won the Nobel Prize for Chemistry in recognition of his work on surface chemistry. The Nobel Committee acknowledged that while others had followed him, the "honour is due to the first man, the pioneer, who has broken new ground." It was a significant comment, offering recognition not only to the recipient but also to his place of employment. Langmuir was neither an academician nor an independent researcher. He was an employee of an industrial research lab, yet he had "broken new ground," as the Nobel Committee had phrased it, in pure science.

After receiving the Nobel Prize, Langmuir encouraged Blodgett to go out on her own and renew the research into surface films that he had largely left behind. She developed her own ideas, along with techniques for building up layers of various films, each being as thin as one molecule in thickness. She knew that because she had developed a special gauge, using the light spectrum to measure the thickness of a surface film. Her work with the color spectrum eventually led her to invent the first nonreflecting glass, which GE introduced in 1938. For the press demonstration, Blodgett treated the glass over a photograph of Whitney, who had by then retired as director of the laboratory. Though the initial version of the antiglare film smudged if it was handled, Blodgett's invention was instrumental in opening the field of industrial coatings and antiglare technology.

If Thomas Edison had proved the value of advanced research in an entrepreneurial setting, GE Research confirmed it in the corporate world. However, while Edison dominated his lab, GE had been successful in allowing individual initiative to find a place in a cooperative setting.

Thomas Edison visited Schenectady in 1922, an august occasion for the General Electric Company. His appearance at his old facility was his first in more than twenty-five years. At the age of seventy-five, he was himself still very much in the business of invention, running his large laboratory in West Orange, New Jersey.

With dozens of reporters and a movie crew in tow, Edison toured the GE Research Lab in Schenectady, still exhibiting the general aura of optimism that had made his assistants at Menlo Park ever willing to work through the night alongside him.

Fittingly, Steinmetz had stayed in his lab long after midnight the night before in anticipation of Edison's visit, readying his own famous invention for creating artificial lightning. The next day Edison started his tour by seeing Coolidge's process for working tungsten into thin wire. He delighted in Langmuir's demonstration of an induction coil—antecedent of the microwave oven—which warmed metal but didn't give off heat. Then he was taken to Steinmetz' lab and saw the artificial lightning, asking to have it repeated under circumstances that he suggested.

During the day in Schenectady, Edison was the guest of honor at a reception in the new corporate headquarters for a handful of his former employees, those who had been with him in the 1880s, when the Machine Works was still new to Schenectady. One of his former managers drew him to a window and pointed to the original buildings. "Remember?" he said, and Edison nodded and smiled.

"Remember that old tower we used to work in?" the aged manager asked, "It stood just beyond there. Remember when we worked three nights on that old dynamo?" Edison laughed.

"Good days," he said.

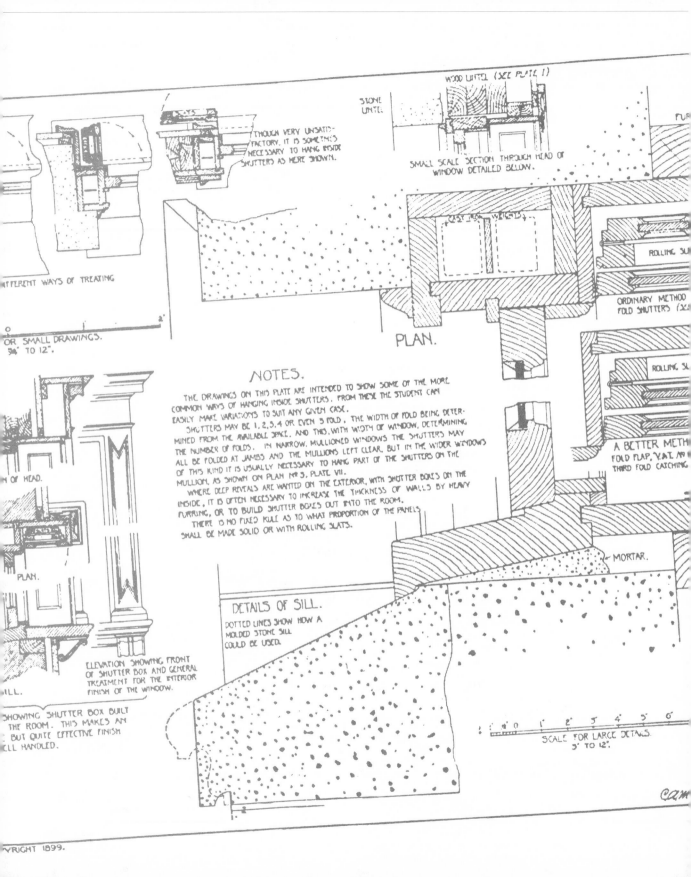

WOOD LINTEL (SEE PLATE 1)

STONE LINTEL

THOUGH VERY UNSATIS-
FACTORY. IT IS SOMETIMES
NECESSARY TO HANG INSIDE
SHUTTERS AS HERE SHOWN.

SMALL SCALE SECTION THROUGH HEAD OF
WINDOW DETAILED BELOW.

CAST IRON WEIGHTS

FUR...

ROLLING SL...

...FFERENT WAYS OF TREATING

...OR SMALL DRAWINGS.
3/8" TO 12".

PLAN.

ORDINARY METHOD
FOLD SHUTTERS (...

ROLLING SL...

A BETTER METH...
FOLD FLAP, V.A... A...
THIRD FOLD CATCHING...

NOTES.

THE DRAWINGS ON THIS PLATE ARE INTENDED TO SHOW SOME OF THE MORE
COMMON WAYS OF HANGING INSIDE SHUTTERS. FROM THESE THE STUDENT CAN
EASILY MAKE VARIATIONS TO SUIT ANY GIVEN CASE.

SHUTTERS MAY BE 1, 2, 3, 4 OR EVEN 5 FOLD, THE WIDTH OF FOLD BEING DETER-
MINED FROM THE AVAILABLE SPACE, AND THIS, WITH WIDTH OF WINDOW, DETERMINING
THE NUMBER OF FOLDS. IN NARROW, MULLIONED WINDOWS THE SHUTTERS MAY
ALL BE FOLDED AT JAMBS AND THE MULLIONS LEFT CLEAR, BUT IN THE WIDER WINDOWS
OF THIS KIND IT IS USUALLY NECESSARY TO HANG PART OF THE SHUTTERS ON THE
MULLION, AS SHOWN ON PLAN Nº 3, PLATE VII.

WHERE DEEP REVEALS ARE WANTED ON THE EXTERIOR, WITH SHUTTER BOXES ON THE
INSIDE, IT IS OFTEN NECESSARY TO INCREASE THE THICKNESS OF WALLS BY HEAVY
FURRING, OR TO BUILD SHUTTER BOXES OUT INTO THE ROOM.

THERE IS NO FIXED RULE AS TO WHAT PROPORTION OF THE PANELS
SHALL BE MADE SOLID OR WITH ROLLING SLATS.

...M OF HEAD.

PLAN.

...HOWING SHUTTER BOX BUILT
...THE ROOM. THIS MAKES AN
...BUT QUITE EFFECTIVE FINISH
...LL HANDLED.

ELEVATION SHOWING FRONT
OF SHUTTER BOX AND GENERAL
TREATMENT FOR THE EXTERIOR
FINISH OF THE WINDOW.

MORTAR.

DETAILS OF SILL.
DOTTED LINES SHOW HOW A
MOLDED STONE SILL
COULD BE USED.

SCALE FOR LARGE DETAILS.
3" TO 12".

CRM

CHAPTER FIVE

The Contagion of Ideas

THE RESEARCH INSTITUTION

As industrial research labs grew larger and larger in the twentieth century, they intimidated many maverick inventors. Complexes of innovation, with the emphasis on *complex*, they were easy to regard as the enemy of the solo inventor, requiring that a person either learn to work in a group setting or else sacrifice the chance to pursue invention on the highest scale. Even Edison expressed his fear that such labs would obviate individual initiative. Yet in practice, quite the opposite came to pass. If labs at their most active had a tendency to grow into veritable armies in the business of ideas, they also had the means to assume the difficult and expensive job of pioneering in the most expansive directions. After that, however, breakthroughs were often abandoned for reasons having nothing to do with potential, or if they were not abandoned, they were left unguarded. Whether because the largest labs were careless, generous, or just oblivious, fields were not only cleared in their wake but left open for individuals and small concerns that added applicable ideas of their own.

On the day that Bell Telephone Laboratories was founded in 1924—following General Electric into the business and the science of the formalized research lab—it already counted two thousand employees. And that figure reflected just the technical staff. The support and management personnel brought the total to eight thousand. Newspaper writers visited Bell Labs' headquarters in New York City, trying desperately to sort out what so many scientists, inventors, and researchers could possibly be doing. They returned to their various newspapers, uniformly overwhelmed by the task.

Bell Labs had two parents: AT&T, the phone service company, and its subsidiary, Western Electric, which manufactured phone equipment. Their respective engineering departments had provided most of the initial personnel for the new Bell Labs. AT&T itself had been founded on invention, of course, and had benefited from unending improvement. Nonetheless, the company seemed to be aware that the world of telephony was still largely a wilderness. The original charter of Bell Labs stipulated that all research was supposed to contribute something of "possible value" to telecommunications. Yet most of modern technology was in some way applicable to the mandate. A description of Bell Labs listed its pursuits as "chemistry, metallurgy, magnetism, electrical conduction, radiation, electronics, acoustics, phonetics, optics, physiology, psychology and meteorology."

It was hard to name the technology that *wouldn't*, in some way, contribute to the ever-modernizing phone system. So it was that Bell Labs looked into practically everything, made advances in much of it, and was thus saddled early on with a reputation as a "dream machine" that couldn't possibly keep up with the potential of its own output.

Through it all, AT&T, the dominant parent, was in a unique position. Major telephone companies in other countries were government-owned. AT&T, however, was a profit-making company as well as a utility. Customers eking out their monthly payments of $1 or $2, and having a hard time doing it, didn't want to hear that the phone company was tossing huge sums into projects of sublime satisfaction only to curious scientists. To quell any such resentment, Bell Labs was organized into four sections. The first, the Research Section, composed of five hundred scientists and technicians, investigated problems posed in telephony. It came the closest of the four to pursuing pure science. The second, the Design Section, took the principles described by the Research Section and turned them into actual inventions. The Systems Section and Engineering Section fit the new inventions into the existing technology.

W. Lincoln Hawkins joined the Research Section in 1942. With a doctorate in chemistry and a unique expertise in plastics, Hawkins was the first African American researcher at Bell Labs. He worked with his colleague, Vincent Lanza, to invent a coating for plastic. It was to be used on all those endless wires, which were, of course, the life matter of most telephony. Previously, phone wires had been coated with lead, which was expensive and heavy but long-lasting. Before Hawkins arrived, the telephone company had great success with plastic, except for the fact that it crumbled apart after less than a year. The Hawkins-Lanza coating, a revolutionary invention in the history of both telephones and plastics, was an example of new research that was handed smoothly through each section at Bell Labs until it was applied in the field, allowing literally millions of far-flung customers to receive telephone service for the first time.

When Karl Jansky arrived at the Research Section in 1928, fresh out of graduate school at the University of Wisconsin, he had a concern

A photo of Karl Jansky from a 1933 Bell Labs press release. He is pointing out radio emission contours on a celestial sky map. The constellations Ursa Major, Ursa Minor, Cassiopeia, and Cygnus are highlighted in his chart.

apart from his interest in electronics: his health. He suffered from chronic kidney problems. As his boss Harald Friis later recalled, Jansky "requested that he be assigned to work which would not exert undue pressure on him." Friis agreed and looked for research that Jansky could pursue at his own pace.

Year in and year out, one of the standing orders in the Research Section was to improve long-distance service. Though earlier long-distance service had been sent through wires, as were local calls, AT&T had managed a remarkable advance in the late teens by implementing radio waves to carry voices and even data (via facsimile machines) across the continent. Broadcast radio was becoming a reality at the same time. The use of long-wave radio in telephony was a tremendous breakthrough, but one that left a tangle of new questions regarding better equipment, more efficient transmission, and most of all, more natural conversations. By the late 1920s, telephone customers had stopped marveling and started complaining. On a typical long-distance call, the line noise was loud, while the voices were faint. That aspect of the service had to be turned around or people would rediscover letterwriting.

Friis ultimately decided that Jansky could start his career at Bell Labs by helping in the effort to reduce the hiss, or white noise, found in long-distance reception. As far as was known at the time, the hiss was caused by static—variations in the electrical charge carrying the radio waves. Bell Labs was looking into a number of ways to eliminate it. First, though, the researchers had to understand static: what it was, how it disturbed the waves, and whence it came. Karl Jansky's assignment pertained to that problem, but it was probably not something he could use to impress his friends at parties. His job was to record static.

To make various recordings and measurements of the static, Jansky inherited an array of equipment, including antennas that were constructed in rows, according to his direction, in a field in central New Jersey. Some of them were placed on an enormous round carriage, which could be turned to adjust the reception. He called it his merry-go-round. By 1931, Jansky knew his static the way other people knew their

Karl Jansky built an antenna, pictured here, designed to receive radiowaves. It was mounted on a turntable that allowed it to rotate.

stamp collections, and he had sorted it into three types: thunderstorms nearby, thunderstorms far away, and one he termed rather vaguely "a steady hiss state." He could identify the popping type of static caused by thunderstorms, either local or long-distance. He couldn't, however, trace the source of the third type, the hissing static. Eventually, he consulted with a colleague at Bell Labs, A. Melvin Skellett, who had been educated as an astronomer. Between the two of them, they concluded that the waves were coming from the Milky Way. The phenomenon that Jansky came to call "star noise" or "galactic waves" was caused by radio waves emanating from turbulence on stars forty thousand light-years away. When Jansky described his breakthrough in 1933, newspapers around the world carried it as important news: the first type of communication, if only ambient, from the far end of the galaxy.

The shy young scientist was a celebrity, betraying his own excitement only a bit when he said that "the discovery of galactic waves raises many questions of extreme interest." Unfortunately, he was to find that he was wrong about the level of interest. After the initial fascination, everyone seemed to return to matters an arm's length away, not forty thousand light-years away. The tale of the announcement was summed up in a headline in the *Syracuse Herald* on May 6, 1933: "Galactic Radio Waves from Outer Space / Mysterious Discovery Announced by Scientists / The Possibility of Signals from Other Worlds / President Calls for Increased Wage Schedules."

While the president dealt with wage schedules, Jansky continued his research. He was listening to the stars, but no one seemed to be listening to him. By 1938, he felt that it was time to move on to other research. Friis was quick to explain, however, that it was not Bell Labs that stopped him: "Karl was free to continue work on star noise if he had wanted to, but more than 5 years had passed since he made his epochal discovery, and not a word of encouragement to continue his work had appeared from scientists or astronomers. They did not understand its significance."

A practical hurdle had arisen as well. "Karl would have needed a large steerable antenna to continue his work," Friis said, "and such antennas were unknown to us at that time."

Such antennas may have been unknown to the celebrated scientists of Bell Labs, but not to the students of Longfellow Grade School in Wheaton, Illinois. In 1938, they were climbing on one for fun after school in the side yard of Grote Reber's house.

Reber was a twenty-six-year-old radio engineer who worked in Chicago and lived in his parents' house in the suburb of Wheaton. He was an average fellow in many respects, cutting the lawn and paying his taxes. Yet he was aware that he was standing on the brink of a new epoch, even in Wheaton, and he was desperate to hurry it along.

Of all the people who had read Karl Jansky's earlier articles, Grote Reber was perhaps the only one who truly understood them and their import. Reber regarded the articles as "an enlightening example of how a first-class mind works." He could see as well as Jansky had, though, that the next step required a larger, more effective antenna. None existed, of course. Reber decided to invent one.

Grote Reber had two things that Bell Labs lacked: an unsinkable belief in radio astronomy and, in part because he could think of little else, a highly original idea for an antenna. Actually, it wasn't entirely original: it was based on a Newtonian observation regarding the properties of a parabola. In Newton's time, a parabola—a curve of potent properties, described according to the laws of calculus—was first used in telescope lenses. Reber adapted it for the same purpose—to "see" the stars—but in an entirely different application. He brought to it the problem of constructing a precise yet easily adjustable radio wave receptor. Over the summer of 1937, he constructed a parabolic dish, 31.4 feet in diameter, which he pointed toward the sky. It was held in place by means of open metalwork, which is what intercepted the school kids. The dish intercepted the waves. They struck its gaping surface and—courtesy of the cunning shape of the parabola—directed them to a point twenty feet above the center of the dish. A barrel-shaped receiver there was positioned to pull them in, amplify them, and then relay them to a listening post inside the house. Once Reber's invention was operational, signals came in more strongly than they ever had through Jansky's array of vertical antennas. Moreover, the whole apparatus could be turned much more easily. As a result, Reber was able to tune in the radio waves more clearly and chart his results even more exactly than Jansky had been able to do.

Reber's invention: the first parabolic radio telescope.

While Reber was using the antenna to intercept the well-traveled radio waves, people around Wheaton were just as busy trying to figure out what the construction in his mother's yard was doing there. People driving past were baffled. So many stopped to inquire that Reber, as he recalled, "considered placing a juke-box out front with a sign, 'Drop quarter in slot and find out what this is all about.'" Jansky hadn't been able to interest even that many people in the new field.

In 1941, Reber made his own try at getting through to the world about radio astronomy. He wrote a well-documented article for the scholarly *Astrophysical Journal*. Reber's results were even more precise than Jansky's had been, owing to his improved antenna. Nonetheless, the editorial board rejected his article, not because of any lack of quality but because they had no use for radio astronomy. However, the editor, Otto Struve, pursued his own investigation, sending astronomers to Wheaton to examine the apparatus and its operation. Ultimately, Struve decided to publish the article and its irrefutable results. During World War II, when most activity in the pure sciences was suspended, Reber continued his research in the side yard and published further data in the *Astrophysical Journal*. A 1944 article offered a map of the skies, showing where the radio waves could be found in the greatest density. Amounting to a how-to kit for tuning in the stars, Reber's article tantalized many scientists. By the time the war ended the following year, radio astronomy was enthusiastically embraced by scientists in the United States, Australia, Britain, and elsewhere. Colleges and government institutions vied for the chance to underwrite new research.

Reber's invention—the first parabolic radio telescope—was soon dwarfed by versions ten times its size and far more sensitive in receiving radio waves. Nonetheless, its rotatable parabolic dish and basic structure are seen in many of the radio telescopes in use today. Reber continued in various scientific pursuits, always remaining as true as possible to his amateur status. For a time though, he had been the caretaker of the art, the only radio astronomer in the world. "The entire enterprise," he said fifty years later, "was a fine adventure in my side yard."

If the industrial research lab managed a delicate balancing act occupying a place somewhere between pure science and practical invention, between individual initiative and cooperation, the formation of the Naval Research Laboratory (NRL) introduced yet another complication: nothing less than the federal government. Before NRL was founded in 1923, the government had never fully been in the business of invention. World War I changed that. Lasting from 1914 to 1918, it was particularly demanding for the United States, a revolution in warfare that served to introduce technology in more new fields than any previous conflict.

The United States wouldn't enter the war until 1917, but over the course of two years before that, the secretary of the navy, Josephus Daniels, was on his guard. Entirely aware of the changes occurring overseas in military methods, he organized the Naval Consulting Board with Thomas Edison as chairman. From 1916 forward, its primary responsibility was identifying inventors with something to contribute to the improvement of military science in general and the navy in particular. First, the board assembled an index card file of people with the knowledge and

Josephus Daniels, secretary of the navy, on Flag Day in Washington, D.C., 1914.

potential to work on advanced research. Next, it identified the most critical military needs. At the top of the list, for example, was a means of finding submarines lurking underwater. The board asked the experts to respond with solutions in the form of new machines or processes.

Harvey C. Hayes was a professor of physics at Swarthmore College in Pennsylvania when the war started in Europe. Knowing of the terror wrought by German U-boats, as in the attack on the ocean liner *Lusitania* in 1915, he took up the study of underwater surveillance on his own initiative, concentrating on the analysis of sound and echo. Several groups in Europe were studying the same possibility. As soon as America entered the war, Hayes contacted the navy, which jumped at the chance to hire him. Moving to New London, Connecticut, with his family, Hayes worked with a team on a rudimentary form of sonar. The word "sonar" would not come into use until the late 1930s, and indeed, the new invention was so shrouded in secrecy that it went without a name for a long time during and after World War I. While the navy was glad to recruit physicists and others with the expertise to invent echo-detecting systems (including radar), it was even more aggressive in signing anyone with real expertise or originality in the field of radiography. Laboratories were hastily organized in order to accommodate the navy's newfound preoccupation with that and other fields of research.

Having collected some of the most inventive minds in the country, the Naval Consulting Board still could not rest. Instead, it did something unique in the annals of invention and the U.S. military: it invited the public to send ideas for machines or processes. All would be seriously evaluated.

"The inventions submitted by the public," wrote Captain Lloyd Scott, an officer attached to the Naval Consulting Board, "which means those inventors who were not immediately connected with the board, not called into consultation by them, amounted to some 110,000." From across the country, people submitted drawings or models related to submarining, bombs, camouflage, periscopes, aircraft, and torpedo defense. Scott reported that the experts who analyzed the submissions passed only one-tenth of 1 percent of them for further testing. With its invitation, however, the navy had let the nation know that a new era was at hand, one in which it needed innovators as much as it needed sailors.

In the peace that followed World War I, the usual procedure would have been for the military to dismantle most of its engineering and development operations, in line with the general reduction in troop strength. Americans were more accustomed to peace than war, and they preferred a small military, which is to say an inexpensive one. After World War I—the war to end all wars (and so on and so forth)—the army and navy were expected to disappear from view. And to a great extent, they did. The navy, however, had been both daunted and enticed by the technological possibilities

Josephus Daniels in his office.

unleashed during the war years: daunted by the threat from submarines and enticed by the use of science. Daniels had no intention of dispersing his carefully culled band of experts.

After the war, Hayes was transferred to the Naval Engineering Station in Annapolis, Maryland, where he continued his work. He was still fascinated with underwater sound: the best way to produce it, detect it, and measure its movement. In 1922, Hayes installed his newest invention, a sonic depth finder, on a U.S. Navy destroyer and sailed with the

John Dove

John Dove was working at Rome Air Development Center (RADC) in the late 1950s, one of about three or four African American engineers at the prestigious research campus. Dove had graduated from Columbia University, and he brought experience in X-ray technology through his work at another government laboratory. RADC was organized to supply the air force with advanced technology in electronics, radars, and communications.

In thinking of potential projects, Dove was far ahead of his time, even at an advanced lab. "One of the things he got into," said his former boss, "was early data processing. In the late 1950s, he was talking about advanced computer techniques, especially memory systems. In those days, things were pretty crude and memory systems were bulky. I remember John saying in about 1960, 'there ought to be some way of storing data and then extracting it from things as small as an atom. You could probably do something to an atom with something as high frequency as ultraviolet light and find out what state it was in—mark it and then read it, so to speak.' It's a negative thing for me to relate because I thought it was just too far advanced and told him so. But he said there was no reason that memory needed to take up so much space. I'll always remember that."

Dove continued to think about his idea, and a few years later, RADC agreed to support his research. The result was technology integral to the compact disc (CD) and related data storage media. Dove's innovation did not utilize UV waves in transcription but rather laser beams. He had the knowledge to hone in on the details of his invention, but more unique was his perspective, seeing further than others early on. Dove continued to produce inventions in the high-technology field and was at work on a fiber optic amplifier when he died in 2004.

crew out into the Atlantic to test it. That was something he could not have done back at Swarthmore. Hayes' apparatus measured the depth of the water by bouncing sound waves off the ocean floor and measuring the elapsed time for the return trip. After a few days at sea, Hayes sent a telegram back to Annapolis, announcing that the depth finder was a "complete success." News of the breakthrough was carried in newspapers all over the country.

Hayes' invention revealed something very significant not only about the contour of the ocean floor but also about a hidden dimension of the navy's research program. He had started out looking to invent a means of finding combatant submarines. Along the way, he developed equipment that helped the navy, of course, but that also redefined two peacetime sciences, oceanography (the study of the underwater landscape) and seismology (the study of disturbances in the landscape). Hayes' depth finder was immediately placed into service mapping the ocean floor, and it was especially helpful in solving ancient mysteries in coastal waters.

Naval research, even in its early days after World War I, was an expensive undertaking, but one that inevitably benefited disciplines far beyond military science. In many cases, an invention emerging from naval research facilities could never have been realized except under the aegis of a government agency with the scope of the navy. Unless Harvey Hayes, for example, had been fortunate enough to inherit a large ocean-going ship from a relative, he would have had a hard time testing an invention as ambitious as the sonic depth finder.

While Hayes was introducing the depth finder, two of his colleagues, Alfred Hoyt Taylor and Leo C. Young, were making observations that would lead to the invention of radar in the 1930s. Throughout the various sections of the navy's research—all remnants of work begun during the war—employees were working areas that veritably demanded further study. As a result of the breadth of the research and its sense of imperative, the Naval Research Laboratory was formally organized as a department within the U.S. Navy in July 1923. The headquarters was in Virginia, across the Potomac from Washington. NRL grew markedly during World War II, when its high-frequency radar system came to be regarded as a critical technology, and afterward, when it took the initiative in advancing German rocket engineering. NRL's Vanguard rocket branch was a primary component of NASA when it was organized in 1958.

NRL, the government's first large-scale foray into the research laboratory, was regarded with suspicion by those who believed that the initiative for invention should come from the human spirit alone—with perhaps an occasional gust of encouragement from the free-market system. In its early days, NRL represented more of a revolution than it would today, when so many inventors are working productively, and apparently comfortably, for the government.

When NRL was formed, the temptation was to condemn government-sponsored invention as a menace. All such research, on its ever-expanding scale, seemed to offer planned innovation as a surrogate for the planned economy that was anathema to most Americans. That the government exercised decisive influence over the course of invention cannot be denied. By the 1950s, approximately 50,000 people were working in various government innovation laboratories; in the early twenty-first century, the number was more than 150,000, making the federal government the largest and certainly most influential of all of the world's invention factories. Without government sponsorship of innovation, both the current state of technology and the current way of life would be very different. Placing such a high priority on innovation, however, the U.S. government also inculcated a culture of invention. It glamorized its own most conspicuous theater of invention, NASA, and made it emblematic of invention as a form of heroism.

The global positioning system (GPS), the marvel of the 1990s that one air force officer called "as important as the invention of the compass," was a success born of government investment at its highest levels.

The Transit satellites of the early 1960s were the earliest operated for navigational purposes. Shown are Transit 1A (left) and Transit 2A with GRAB-1 Satellite (right). In use until the early 1990s, Transit technology was developed by the Johns Hopkins Applied Physics Laboratory, one of many research organizations that deserve a measure of credit for the realization of the GPS.

The Timation satellite, developed at the Naval Research Laboratory, was the precursor of the modern Navstar satellite used in today's GPS system.

The idea of using satellites in navigation occurred to a number of scientists in the mid-1950s. Over the course of the next generation, groups with vast resources pursued it, each taking the lead at different points. The Aerospace Corporation, a research institute originally launched by the air force, developed the framework and formulas to operate a system. NRL performed its own preliminary studies in conjunction with the Johns Hopkins Applied Physics Laboratory and put them into use with the launch of its Transit satellites in 1960 and more sophisticated Timation satellites in the late 1960s. The air force had developed a program of its own, directed at perfecting an accurate, universal system, and in 1972 it joined forces with the navy in realizing the full potential of the idea of global positioning.

The venture, called Navstar, drew on refinements from research arms within both services, as well as academic laboratories and the industrial labs of companies such as Rockwell International, Raytheon, and Frequency & Time Systems, a pioneer manufacturer of atomic clocks. The effort represented the culmination of the very concept of the research laboratory.

The system requires twenty-four satellites to provide global coverage. Each one is in constant communication with fixed tracking stations on Earth so that it always has a digital record of its own location. It also has the time, give or take one second every thirty thousand years, courtesy of an onboard atomic clock. Receiving a signal from one of the orbitting Navstar satellites, a GPS unit on the ground—also equipped with an

Milstar Satellite Communications System, commonly known as GPS.

THE SPIRIT OF INVENTION

atomic clock—can calculate the distance between them, based on the amount of time that the signal was en route. Signals from three Navstar satellites, combined with speedy calculations by a small computer, allow a GPS unit to determine its own location. Typically, however, pinpoint accuracy depends on communication with as many as eight Navstar satellites. The process of launching the satellites started in 1978. Until the full complement was in orbit, the service was quite limited, but in 1995, the system was finally declared complete and operational. Even then the military asserted its priority, and civilian use was checked by the knowledge that the armed services could scramble GPS signals at any time. In 1996, President Bill Clinton, acting on a promise originally made by President Ronald Reagan, directed that the system be opened permanently to the general population around the world. His statement was tantamount to an invitation to inventors everywhere to take up GPS and find ways to use it. It may not have been as overt an invitation as the one the Naval Consulting Board had issued eighty years before, but it had the same effect: inspiring people with sophisticated training and those with no training at all to put ideas into materials and create something practical and perhaps exciting for the world.

In 1996, President Bill Clinton opened the GPS system to the general population around the world.

An emergency room doctor was one of the first to suggest putting GPS receivers in cell phones so that accident victims could be located. His idea, however, was an example of the right idea at the wrong time. In the late 1990s, phone companies were reluctant to adopt any tracking capability because of legal concerns over privacy issues. In other words, people did not want to be connected to Big Brother. After the attacks on September 11, 2001, however, attitudes turned around completely. Indeed, people wanted to feel connected—to a source of help, to Big Brother, to anyone. The Federal Communications Commission ultimately mandated the implementation of GPS receivers in cell phones, but only to the extent of allowing emergency services to locate a caller in the event of a 911 call.

Inventors implemented GPS technology in dog collars and on wristbands for children or others likely to get lost. An inventor in southern

PARC

When Xerox opened its Palo Alto Research Center (PARC) in 1970, the computer industry was still insulated from the everyday world. Access to computers was limited, and using one was an alien experience, requiring knowledge of unfamiliar operating languages along with a pronounced dexterity with punch cards. PARC, however, came to digital electronics with a different attitude: that computers, like all its products (like photocopiers, to be specific), should be easy to use and impossible to live without.

PARC's first director, George Pake, recruited inventive people from a variety of fields. His goal, as he later wrote, was "to maintain in close association under one roof the physical sciences and the computer sciences." A colleague had a livelier impression of Pake's management style: "He knew what you had to do was get the very best people and let them go follow their ideas."

PARC's first success was the development of the laser printer, which itself led to laser scanning optics, character generation electronics, and page-formatting software. None of that was a far throw from Xerox's home turf in duplicating machines, but then, PARC had only begun to spew inventions. Early on, the center dedicated itself to a highly original idea: "an experiment in personal computing," as its own employees expressed it in a research paper, "to study how a small, low-cost machine could be used to replace facilities then provided only by much larger shared systems." To most veterans of the computer industry, that smacked of the absurd—until 1973, when PARC employees invented Alto.

The Alto personal computer was a desktop before that term was coined. As a snapshot of the future, it lacked for little. Alto came with a graphical user interface (GUI) display screen, inculcating what the inventors called "windows" (the quotes are theirs). It employed a keyboard and a mouse, although the mouse had actually been invented three years before at the Stanford Research Institute.

Alto was specifically designed for "interacting with a user and satisfying his needs." Previously, computers had been created for the sake of the task, not the user. Alto could handle interactive programming, animation, and music. And needless to say, it was attached to a laser printer. There was more. If one Alto was a boon, two or more created a world without horizons. PARC engineers connected their personal computers and originated an e-mail system. They also invented the Ethernet and created a working Internetwork, as it was termed then, with its own servers and a protocol called PUP. Other personal computers began to emerge by the mid-1970s, but none was as complete as Alto—or as prepared for the future. Nonetheless, personal computing eventually forged ahead without Alto and without Xerox itself taking a major role.

Xerox inventors consistently shared their breakthroughs, through published papers and seminar talks. In establishing a research center, especially in the fluid atmosphere of an academic community, a company risks that it will give away as much as it gets in the going currency of ideas. In the case of PARC, Xerox took the short end of that bargain, but it did create an institution that was a national treasure in its heyday and a boon to invention far beyond its walls.

California introduced an accessory for a golf cart that could describe the direction and exact distance to the flag from the tee, the fairway, or the very deep rough. Inventors worked on ways to implement GPS into computer-generated speech devices to guide the blind through unfamiliar streets.

Of all of the modern inventions, the GPS is the one that would be most astonishing to people in the past, and it is something of a pleasure to imagine oneself casually explaining it to the likes of Thomas Jefferson or Cleopatra, or just a farm family on the steppes of Russia. Who could fail to be amazed by the convergence of inventions—satellites, atomic clocks, computers, and radios—into a system that ensures that a person simply cannot get lost ever again—unless the thing is recalculating, of course.

Research laboratories accelerated innovation, granting power to corporations and governments to create a mainstream of invention. That the individual inventor continued to thrive in or near the giant research labs may have been a surprise to those who eyed such institutions warily when creativity was at stake. The mileu of invention has not necessarily changed, not even since the sash saw was refined into the muley and then replaced by the seminal band saw. No one person is responsible for the creation of the GPS, either, a prime example of an invention that depended on the brilliance of many and so credits the anonymous inventor in the modern age.

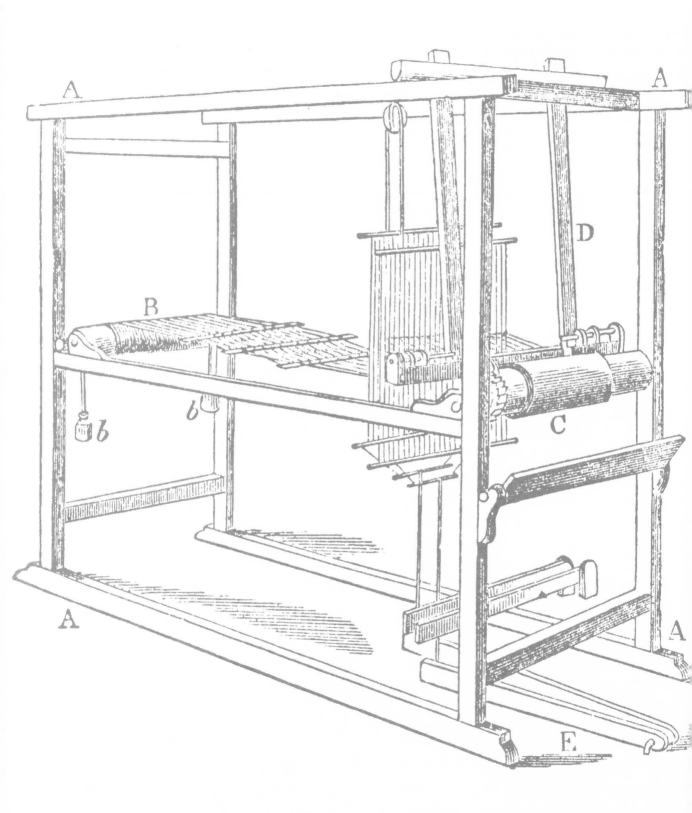

THE WORLD AND THE INVENTOR

The glorious history of invention also happens to be the history of annoyance, impatience, and aggravation. Placid contentment doesn't tend to foment change. An invention is almost necessarily predicated by a person who is sick and tired of something or other.

A tendency for irritation is one of the inventor's keenest assets. It identifies potential inventions like a light beam and veritably leaves a to-do list, or more pointedly, a to-invent list. The quality of annoyance has curious properties as a form of fuel: in the case of labor-saving devices, an inventor who is too lazy to do a job the old way will press on with endless energy in seeking an improvement.

According to the medical dictionary, irritation is a response to outside stimuli—such as those carried through the senses. And it is the senses that form the first bridge between the imagination and actuality. Inventors devote their lives to dominating that bridge. It is as though the gods created one world and human invention has never stopped creating another within and around the first.

The senses, which are the primary form of organization for the inventor's mind, also form the structure in the section to follow. Different people are more sensitive to the stimuli of one sense over another, of course. The Lemelson Center has pioneered the study of invention in relation to color and music. The attention is well placed, with both color and music having inspired inventors from prehistoric times up to the very present.

The chapters herewith take a perch on those bridges, the major senses, to look at the ways they draw inventors over, giving them no choice but to drop all else and fix what only they can see—or hear or feel or taste.

 **CHAPTER SIX**

The Palette of the Inventor

COLOR AS THE MEDIUM

*I*n the mid-1980s, old Hollywood arose again. Its heroes squinted into the bright lights and walked once more before the cameras. They may have been wizened and weak, but they were still heroic, taking on a fight that grew more ferocious than anyone might first have predicted.

Fifty years before, the American movie industry had ruled an empire of the imagination that stretched all the way around the world. Producers turned out movies quickly and with comparative ease, with an artistic emphasis on storytelling that has led to the 1930s and 1940s being regarded as the classic era of filmmaking. Ginger Rogers sang and danced, sometimes with Fred Astaire, in gleaming art deco settings. James Stewart was carefully nurtured into stardom through a wide variety of roles, from historical drama to the sophisticated comedy of *The Philadelphia Story*.

Each studio, in Hollywood's heyday, was created to be as autonomous as possible, containing all the various experts needed to produce movies by the hundreds each year. Somehow, the movie lots managed to combine the contrasting viewpoints of art and industry and draw them into an efficient process. The stars might prove temperamental, the directors might dither, but armies of technical specialists kept busy and kept to the schedule. And in the midst of it all, one aspect of the system was entirely predictable: the film itself. Because black-and-white film was simple to process, it was inexpensive to use, encouraging studios to make more films. Directors had long since learned to love its surprising possibilities, ranging from the shaded style of Richard Boleslavsky to the crisp, even resplendent, imagery of Ernst Lubitsch in a musical such as *The Merry Widow*. In the hands of masters, black and white delineated moods, if not hues, with an endless palette.

By the 1980s, the old Hollywood movies should have been long gone, relegated to an archive for the sake of history. But something unexpected had happened, perhaps because so much care had been taken with productions at the studios. Movies that had originally been produced for the sake of a run of a few weeks were still remembered and beloved fifty years later. In 1986, Ted Turner, the television mogul, paid $1.4 billion for a library of movies from the heyday of MGM and Warner Bros. Other television executives felt sorry for him, calling the deal a waste of money. They supported that position by pointing to marketing surveys, which held that 85 percent of all potential viewers (and, statistically, 100 percent of those under the age of twenty) would refuse to watch any black-and-white movies. Turner had just purchased 3,650 of them. Known to be unsinkable, Turner nonetheless seemed a bit nervous about his new hoard of monochrome classics. A solution, however, was at hand.

In 1983, a Canadian engineer named Wilson Markle had unveiled a computer-assisted technique for updating the old movies. During the silent era, a few movies and short subjects had been hand-tinted, but

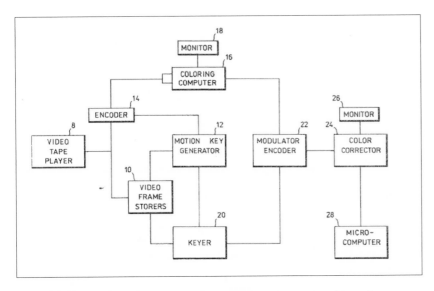

Wilson Markle and Brian Holmes invented the colorization process for motion pictures. This schematic diagram reflects the process of reorganizing the movie and then applying—or "keying"—color into similar frames.

that wasn't even considered in modern times. The average movie contains 200,000 frames. Employing artists to hand-tint that many separate images would be astronomically expensive.

Markle headed a team that had invented colorization—a means of electronically adding tint to a film. In the process, a black-and-white film was transferred to video and then completely reordered, so that all of the frames from the same scene were grouped together. An art director assigned colors to the various surfaces depicted in the first and last frame of each scene; computers, with the help of another technician, continued those color schemes throughout the intervening frames. The challenge was teaching the computer to recognize the same basic patterns, even though they shifted slightly with the motion depicted in the film. The success of the process depended on the addition of a "motion indicator key," as Markle's patent application explained:

Since only a small percentage of each frame changes from one frame to another, once one frame has had colors assigned to each dot or pixel of the frame, corresponding dots or pixels in the next frame can be assigned the same color, and changes of color are only required to be made to areas corresponding to areas of motion. This significantly reduces the number of operations required to color a black and white motion picture.

The Markle invention, and others that followed, required artists to specify the colors in only about a thousand of the frames. The balance was handled by computers, guided all the while by the motion indicator key and a supervising technician. It wasn't a simple process, but it was an improvement on hand-tinting.

Markle's company, eventually called Colorization, Inc., forecast that its market would lie in television, where syndication made valuable properties of even the most tired repeats. That is, the color repeats were valuable because black-and-white shows were harder to sell to a generation raised on color programming. Colorization, however, ultimately proved to be too expensive to use for television shows. That left movies. The owners of the Hal Roach Studio in California invested heavily in Markle's company, ordering new versions of several Laurel and Hardy movies. "Every time we went to sell something," said the studio's chairman, referring to the rights to broadcast a particular movie, "they'd say, 'Well, this is only worth so much, because it's black and white.' So we thought, well, if these pictures were in color, they'd command a much bigger price."

The Roach Studio, though hardly Hollywood's largest, owned the rights to a 1936 comedy called *Topper,* starring Constance Bennett, Cary Grant, and Roland Young. It became the first full-length movie to be colorized. The second was *Miracle on 34th Street* with Maureen O'Hara and John Payne. When it was broadcast in 1985, the ratings seemed to prove the marketing studies right: viewership was four times larger than it had been in previous years for the black-and-white version of the Christmas movie. At the same time, *Topper* underscored the new wisdom that color gave fresh life to old movies. After languishing for years as a relic interesting only to film buffs, *Topper* earned $2 million in its first year-and-a-half as a newly minted color film.

Ted Turner bypassed Markle's company but leapt at the chance to hire a similar laboratory, Color Systems Technology, to work its magic on his film library, starting with the adaptation of one hundred classic movies. Turner didn't go into such things in a small way, however. While *Topper* and *Miracle on 34th Street* were movies of secondary interest to most film buffs, the list of films that Turner intended to update started with nothing less than *The Maltese Falcon*, directed by John Huston. It was in the first tier of Hollywood movies, a landmark in the cynical urban genre known as film noir. With great fanfare, the debut of the enhanced *Maltese Falcon* was announced for broadcast on TBS on November 12, 1986.

Huston, the vigorous sportsman who had directed the picture, came forward at the age of eighty to protest. Confined to a wheelchair and breathing with difficulty despite the oxygen tank at his side, Huston explained in a news conference the following day that he had tuned into the program. "I looked for as long as I could bear it," he said, "I asked myself if such an example of mindless insipidity is worthy of our attention."

Director John Huston, when he protested colorization of *The Maltese Falcon*.

It was only a movie, though, and movies had been corrupted for decades, as a matter of course, in order to fit into television schedules. They'd been converted to video with its coarse texture. They'd been chopped up and reedited to allow for commercials. A few people groused when such liberties were taken, but nothing that had come before matched the reaction to the colorized version of *The Maltese Falcon*—unless it was the outcry that greeted the colorized version of Frank Capra's *It's a Wonderful Life*, or the war that erupted at even the thought of changing *Casablanca*.

Directors by the score voiced their rage at the sheer hubris of tampering with the artwork of others. None of the contemporary directors, though, carried the weight of the people who had made that art in its day. James Stewart and Ginger Rogers led a contingent of veteran Hollywood stars to Washington to testify at congressional hearings over the issue. Capra, well into his eighties, had preceded them with an impassioned letter to the Library of Congress. He had originally endorsed the idea of colorization but changed his mind. He explained why, from the point of view of the artist behind the making of *It's a Wonderful Life*:

> I chose to shoot it in black-and-white film. The lighting, the makeup for the actors and actresses, the camera and laboratory work, all were geared for black-and-white film, not color. I beseech you with all my heart and mind not to tamper with a classic in any form of the arts. Leave them alone. They are classics because they are superior. Do not help the quick money-makers who have delusions about taking possession of classics by smearing them with paint.

A scene from *It's a Wonderful Life*, with Donna Reed, James Stewart, and Karolyn Grimes.

The battle raged throughout 1986 and 1987. Few people didn't have an opinion, and most of them, in Hollywood at least, were indignantly opposed to the new versions of the old classics. On Capitol Hill, Stewart called colorization "cultural butchery." Wilson Markle couldn't understand that response. He tried to defend his invention. "The eye doesn't recognize black-and-white," he insisted. "It occurs nowhere in nature. We're not altering black and white. We're enhancing it."

The anger centered around just one factor, easily overlooked and yet intrinsic to all perception: color. The right color speaks into the mind without words. In the eighteenth century, color was regarded as medicine and the rooms of patients were painted different colors depending on the illness to be cured. In modern times, the effect of color and its near relative, light, have been found to bear a direct correlation to mental health. Designers and decorators devote their days to understanding the spectrum in minute detail. On a purely practical basis, though, color represents an enticing challenge for the inventor. While shades of various hues define the way that most people see what is before them, color allows inventors to reach out into the world. It is a medium all its own, inspiring them to find ways to control it, adding to its possibilities and to its uses.

Eventually, colorization of classic movies lost most of its appeal. Pressure from the federal government certainly discouraged it, but audience disapproval had an even greater effect. The novelty wore off, and ratings returned to approximately the same level garnered by uncolorized versions of the same movies. The outrage didn't fade though. The impassioned response to the colorization of classic movies stood as proof that the reality of tint or hue is not a mere question of preference. It

Frank Capra, director of *It's a Wonderful Life.*

is quite literally a smack in the eye. As with the other senses, vision pulls the world inside the mind, where color immediately becomes aligned with emotion. It can even be emotion as soon as it is absorbed. Color is capable of delighting, of course, but of infuriating as well, able to inspire and/or repel. Inventors were naturally attracted to so powerful a force.

Henry Ford sold millions of Model T's, and it is well known that the vast majority of them were black—as in the apocryphal sales line "You can have one in any color you want, as long as it's black." As a matter of fact, all mass-produced cars in the years around 1920 offered the same wide choice of either black or else black. Colorful paints cost a great deal of money to apply and typically didn't wear well. Ford assumed that the situation didn't have to change; in terms of allure, he regarded a Model T as other people looked at a wheelbarrow—it didn't much matter what color it was as long as it kept rolling.

General Motors, however, would put an end to the Model T, in part by appealing to the yearning for color. GM was controlled in large measure by Dupont, where laboratory scientists had invented colorful automotive lacquers in the early 1920s: on July 4, 1920, to be exact, when an experiment with a nitrocellulose pencil lacquer went awry. Before cleaning it up, Dupont technicians noticed that the substance

Charles Kettering.

was capable of retaining an unusually intense amount of pigment. With cooperation from Charles Kettering at General Motors, the lacquer, named Duco, eventually changed the look of the road, starting with the 1924 "True Blue" Oakland. All General Motors cars were offered in a choice of colors by 1926. Customers understood the language of color, with its promise of the quality of newness. By the time Ford offered its Model T in an array of colors, it was too late. Eighteen years after it was introduced, the flivver still looked old. And even in baby blue, it still looked black.

Just as mass-produced cars were expected to be black—and for many years, they were—cotton was for a long time expected to be white. In ancient cultures, tinted cotton was highly valued, but modern times looked upon it as a blight. In fact, the United States and other nations around the world actively discouraged cultivation of any plants containing a natural tint, in the belief that agriculture and industry would both be better with unadulterated breeding. White cotton, after all, could be dyed any color the market demanded. A. W. Brabham, a wealthy planter near Savannah, Georgia, had a different notion of what would be best. He believed that the whole process could be simplified if the cotton came in colors from the start.

For years, Brabham studied cottons of the world. In 1911, he began to grow imported plants in a careful program of selection. Four years later, bolls of Brabham's new cottons were displayed on a board at the Cotton Exchange in Savannah. His fellow growers were impressed to see cotton on the stalk in tan, yellow-green, light brown, olive green, and bronze. "The samples," commented a reporter, "can not by any stretch of the imagination be confused with tinges in cotton which might be the result of exposure or weather conditions. Neither is there any suspicion that dyes have been used to produce the colors."

Brabham took his display home and kept working. His bronzes and olive greens were intriguing but useless as far as his fellow planters were concerned. Brabham kept working, cultivating his plants and coaxing them to grow in distinctive shades. His goal wasn't color, however. In

The cover of the August 1926 issue of *Motor* magazine spoofed the new interest in color paints for cars.

the world he occupied, the only cotton that would compete with white was jet black. It would find an instant market since the vast majority of clothes in Brabham's day were either black or white. Over the following seventeen years, Brabham managed to grow fields of blue cotton, but the most valuable strain he cultivated was not botanical at all: it was the strain of serious interest shown by the U.S. government in his experiments. In 1932, a representative of the government's Bureau of Plant Industry made an appointment to visit Brabham's plantation to examine his methods and his results. Brabham was confident that he was on the verge of his lifelong goal, the invention of a method for growing black cotton. Just days before the government botanist arrived, A. W. Brabham died. After his death, his colored cotton fields were ignored and abandoned in an era that just didn't want anything but white.

Nearly fifty years later, the search for a practical colored cotton resumed through the curiosity of a Californian named Sally Fox. Educated as a biologist, she was working on a farm in 1981, helping to develop an insect-resistant strain of cotton, when she came across a bag of seeds supplied by the research department of the Department of Agriculture, seeds that produced brown cotton, according to the label. Having never heard of naturally colored cotton, Fox was intrigued. Her bosses on the farm had no interest in brown cotton, but she decided to try the seeds in the only plantation she had: her mother's backyard. Like Brabham, Fox was hooked on the dream of developing strains of colored cotton. Unlike her predecessor, she had the good fortune to be working on the problem in an era friendly to natural products. As she found larger tracts for her project, she was able to sell raw cotton to individual spinners and weavers.

The process of dyeing fabric involves toxins, as Fox knew all too well. She was personally acquainted with the case of a woman who had taught courses in dyeing fabric until she sustained serious brain damage from the chemicals absorbed through her skin. The dangers of dye inspired Fox to embrace her quest with a kind of passion and the goal of bypassing the poisons to let cotton bring its own color to fabrics. As a parallel benefit, naturally colored cotton tended to be resistant to pests, obviating another toxic problem, the heavy use of pesticides in the cultivation of white cotton.

Fox's work started with brown cotton, but it didn't end there. She crossed plants of the original tint with white strains and produced an attractive green cotton. "It allowed me to realize that if green could come out of brown, yellow could come out of brown, red could come out of brown, many colors could come out of brown. And maybe blue could come out of green." As Fox developed productive seeds, she patented them. She also honed methods that ensured that the plantings would result in the long-staple cotton required by industrial spinning machines. "A lot of what I breed," she said, "is not just color, but farmability."

Sally Fox in her Arizona cotton fields.

To breed a new cotton plant requires between seven and ten years. Ultimately, Fox was able to offer about a half dozen colors, essentially the same ones isolated by Brabham generations before, though she added a russet shade to the bronzes and greens. In the early 1990s, Fox found herself at the center of exploding demand for naturally colored cotton. "You've got a lot of people who are environment crazed," said a Georgia farmer who had recently planted ninety acres of russet-colored cotton. "They want everything natural." The resolve to buy naturally colored cotton alternated with a reluctance to pay extra for the opportunity. Demand for naturally colored cotton has ebbed and flowed over the years, but the niche was established, largely through Fox's innovative breeding. The miracle fabric that had been around for four thousand years was not likely to be forgotten again.

Inventors are drawn to opportunity, of course, as they see it. They were drawn to black, as in flivvers, and white, as in bales of cotton—with a sense of missionary zeal, adding color where it did not exist before.

That attitude, however, did not take hold immediately at the firm of Binney & Smith, located in the lower Hudson River valley of New York State. During the 1890s the company made lampblack and was contented in pursuit of the blackest of the black in good black lampblacks. A pigment used by artists and inkmakers, lampblack was originally gathered from the soot clinging to fixtures lit by burning oil. Messrs. Binney and Smith—first cousins—were moderately successful in their quiet business. Then C. Harold Smith, a gregarious man by nature, did something especially radical for a company in the business of black. He went to England and brought home the rights to a new type of red oxide, a prime ingredient of paint. Edwin Binney, for one, was delighted to look at something other than black. The company energetically promoted the product to paint manufacturers, who promoted it in turn to farmers. As a result, Binney & Smith claimed credit for its part in changing the American landscape when its pioneering and inexpensive "barn red" became the color that marked the family farm.

The promulgation of barn red didn't represent innovation on the company's part, only clever marketing. Through an association with a family named Ketchum, owners of a talc mine in North Carolina, Binney & Smith started to make chalk for use in schools. It claimed a breakthrough in developing a dustless yellow chalk for use on the blackboard: a minor invention, perhaps, but one that apparently cleared the nation's schoolrooms of billows of chalk pollution, especially on days when the more intricate math equations were worked out on the board.

Edwin Binney and C. Harold Smith, creators of Crayola crayons.

The association with schoolchildren led company representatives to realize that the crayons of the day were really not much fun. In fact, they were annoying, which is hardly a characteristic that should belong to crayons. The wax pigment was typically as hard as a rock, one that stubbornly refused to leave much more than a faintly tinted scratch on a piece of paper. W. L. Ketchum was part of the team that had already invented a thick kind of crayon for use marking boards in lumberyards. With experience in making lumber crayons, Binney & Smith had only to find ways to make safe (even edible) colored versions for use by children. Ketchum went on to create a series of appealing crayons, though each color represented a fresh challenge in terms of tint and density. Even in an office memo, his description of the recipe kept the ingredients secret. "In making the #29 Red Lumber crayon," he wrote, "we first mix our pigments, such as the reds, 'B,' 'M,' and 'K' in the ball mixing machine."

The new crayon was introduced in 1903. It was a success from the first, easy to hold and to use. As children through the years demanded greater variety, the company responded, producing colors by the hundreds, in sets containing as many as ninety-six different crayons. The first colors, the ones that started the children drawing, were quite basic: three primary colors (red, yellow, and blue), three secondary colors (orange, purple, and green), one neutral color (brown), and, of course, a good black.

First box of eight Crayola crayons, 1903.

For Robert Switzer, those colors would have been just a bit too timid. He was determined to invent new ways to stretch the power of color. He started in an unlikely way, with an accident that might easily have killed him.

In 1932, Bob Switzer was nineteen years old, a student at the University of California at Berkeley who made a hobby of performing magic tricks.

Working a part-time job at Safeway, the grocery chain, he was unloading crates of food from a boxcar when he stumbled and fell against the railroad ties, striking his head on one of the rails. The blow put him into a coma. Months later, he was still unconscious.

When Switzer finally awoke, his doctor advised that his room be kept dark for the sake of his convalescence. Whatever had gone before, Switzer's mind was soon back to normal, and with nothing to look at, he was bored. The one thing that he could see was the glow from a box of fluorescent rocks that he kept in his room. As he played with them, he switched on a black light, a type of lamp that emits ultraviolet rays but no visible light. The fluorescent material in the rocks absorbed the energy transmitted by the UV rays and emitted it in the form of intensely colored visible light. The rocks in Switzer's room turned gaudy and gorgeous. They weren't bright enough to interfere with his condition, but they did give him a great deal to think about.

Pondering the way that the rocks glowed while the rest of the room remained dark, the young Switzer grew fascinated—not as a young scientist, but as a magician. As soon as he was allowed to stand up and walk around, he took action on the invention he'd thought through in the dark of his sickroom. He mixed fluorescent particles with clear varnish, using the family bathtub for his experiments. (This was his only mistake; his mother took one look and forbade him to bring the chemicals into the house ever again.) Undaunted, Bob Switzer then enlisted his brother, Joe, also an amateur magician, to design tricks using the glow-in-the-dark paint. They weren't amateurs for long, however. In 1934, they began to sell their newly designed tricks. In a sales letter sent to a performer named Kleeland the Magician, the brothers described their invention:

> We are manufacturing a number of magical illusions that are most startling and weird. The Balinese dancer appears on a dark stage in a flash of brilliant light and dances in a strange manner. For the climax, she twists her body in agony and raises her glowing hands with long

Robert Switzer.

fluorescent fingernails as she draws her head off her shoulders. She continues to dance but falls slowly to the floor. Her head continues to move about the stage. This illusion can be packaged in a small bag and sent to you for $75.

The Switzers abandoned college and moved to Ohio to pursue the possibilities of fluorescent paint on a full-time basis. The development of fluorescent inks for use in lithography gave them the resources to continue working on yet more inventions. One project, which they kept secret, was a process for bringing out the intensity of fluorescent colors in sunlight—even without a black light. The ultraintense oranges, yellows, and greens that resulted were termed "Day-Glo" by the brothers. During World War II, the Switzers' process was classified as an official war secret, while their paints and dyes were used extensively to mark runways and extend signaling capabilities at sea.

In 1947, Day-Glo was patented, leading to licensing for more than four thousand products by 1954. In fact, Day-Glo was an invention that spawned hundreds of other inventions, from brightly lit, if nonelectric, Christmas trees to bathing suits that were all but guaranteed to draw attention. Day-Glo paints were everywhere, but they were hard to describe. One customer said that they did for color "what the new masters did to the old masters." Art historians might chafe at the implication that there was anything lacking in the old masters, but then, there was nothing lacking in plain, everyday colors, either—until Day-Glo fired them up and tinged them with a hint of the impossible. Trying to imagine a new color is one of the conundrums that reveals the pitiful limits of the human mind. But Day-Glo came close. That is what made 59 percent of people, according to a company study, look twice when it was first introduced.

Day-Glo paints helped to usher in an era of brash, bright colors after World War II. While even a first-year psychology student might be able to connect the need for renewal with the embrace of startling colors, inventors and many designers had yet another inspiration. The plethora of new materials produced during the years of fighting opened possibilities that had never existed before. The fascination with materials and the inclination to add color—the attitudes of the inventor and that of the designer, respectively—combined to produce pivotal results in the Eames Office.

The Eames Office consisted largely of Charles and Ray Eames, a married couple with a famously self-assured knack for designing unfettered furniture. Charles had started out as an architect and Ray had been a painter, but in their work together, they met somewhere in the middle and became designers. During World War II, they spearheaded experiments with plywood. Most people react to plywood by nailing it to a frame of some sort, enforcing its very flatness, but the Eameses took the root of the word—*ply*—as a verb, not a noun. Using the time-honored tradition of inventors everywhere, they made their first experiments in the bathtub in their own house, soaking plywood until it could be shaped. The two of them worked meticulously on the details of the process, choosing the best types of wood, the

Ray and Charles Eames.

thicknesses, the glues, and the temperatures at which to soak the wood. Charles ultimately invented a heated mold. The result was that the Eameses learned to make a compound curve in plywood, rounding it in more than one direction, as though it were a slab of wet clay. No one had ever been able to make plywood so compliant before.

Ray and Charles Eames on the newly constructed steel frame of the Eames House, 1949.

Ray and Charles Eames in their living room, 1958.

The Eameses' home and office complex, located on a hillside overlooking the ocean in Pacific Palisades, California.

Headlights without Pain

One night in 1919, the lights of an oncoming car momentarily blinded an otherwise careful automobile driver. The same thing had happened on roads all over the world before, and it has occurred countless times every night since. Light emanates from headlamps in a chaotic pattern, with some of the errant rays finding their way deep into the eyes of an oncoming driver. In response, most people blink through a long flash of blurry glare. For the driver in the 1919 incident, steering without vision proved tragically impossible. The car crashed, killing a passenger named Mary Chubb.

Mary's husband, Lewis Chubb, was an electrical engineer who responded to the catastrophe by designing a new kind of headlight, one that would reduce glare through the use of a polarizing material. Chubb patented his idea in 1920, but in truth, he was still lacking one ingredient: the polarizing material.

Two years later, thirteen-year-old Edwin Land began to work on the problem of headlight glare. He was inspired by a near collision caused by glare that occurred one night when he was at summer camp. At twenty-five, in 1934, he formally introduced the invention that resulted from his obsessive research: Polaroid, the world's first effective polarizer. It consisted of a clear film coated with tiny crystals that trained light and redirected enough of it to prevent glare.

Companies immediately helped Land turn Polaroid from a concept into a thriving corporation of the same name, finding uses for his invention in cameras, sunglasses, and three-dimensional filmmaking. But Land was still interested most of all in using his material to reduce the problem of glare from automobile headlights. In public demonstrations, he showed that glare could be entirely eradicated with a system encompassing both windshields and headlights. In fact, from behind a polarized windshield, similarly treated headlights appeared as nothing more arresting than a pair of softly blueish discs. It was an elegant solution to a deadly problem.

With safety experts predicting that the use of polarized coatings would save "many thousands of lives" each year, Land was sure that state legislatures would mandate his system. He was wrong. Critics contended that the new headlights would prove to be particularly blinding for drivers who didn't have coated windshields. They were wrong about that, but they also pointed out, correctly, that the nonglare system would add about 0.5 percent to the cost of an average car. In the midst of the Depression, no one was much interested in forging a revolution in automaking, not one that cost money.

During the last half of the 1940s, however, a unique opportunity presented itself. Because automaking had been effectively suspended during World War II, a generation of new models was set to sweep onto the roads afterward. A revolution was not only inevitable but warmly anticipated. Land enthusiastically reintroduced his no-glare system. The auto industry studied it and then studied it some more, but never made any serious attempt to implement it.

Edwin Land made his mark in 1948 by introducing another of his inventions, instant photography. And so it was that the postwar years came and went: the best chance in automobile history to implement Land's invention and take the white daggers out of the night for drivers was lost.

A navy contract for formfitted leg splints encouraged further experiments. They could have made sculpture from their sinuous wood, and they did, but by nature, they were more practical. As a result, in 1945, the Eameses invented the plywood chair, a low-cost yet sleek form of seating.

Charles Eames was particularly interested in designing furniture, while Ray was moved by the tints and hues that greeted her eyes at

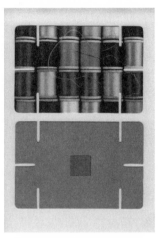

Above are four examples from the Eameses' Giant House of Cards, a building toy for children or adults. Produced in vibrant color, they reflected the way that Ray Eames, in particular, delighted in color and transferred it from everyday objects into stunning design. Each card measures 7 x 4 1/2 inches.

any given moment. She literally collected colors, keeping samples and swatches in her office, while avidly looking to flowers for further ideas. "She liked," wrote the architect Joseph Giovannini, who knew Ray Eames, "the intense orange-red-to-hot-red geranium flower's relationship to its green leaf." In the late 1940s, the Eameses' designs for furniture were rendered in fiberglass, yet another material developed during the war. Fiberglass accommodated their trademark compound curves. Eames side chairs and the even more spare stacking chairs were stylish yet inexpensive. They soon became ubiquitous in offices, waiting rooms, and meeting halls. They remained fresh, however, in part because the fiberglass encouraged the use of color—something with which inexpensive furniture had never bothered before.

Though Charles Eames had been trained as an architect, he did not build many houses in his later years. The most notable example is the Eameses' own home and office complex, located on a hillside overlooking the ocean in Pacific Palisades, California. Consisting of two box-shaped structures connected by a walk, the place was constructed almost entirely of industrial materials. Charles bragged that the cost of construction was less than one-tenth that of a house made of traditional materials. The result is not industrial, though, but airy and inviting. One of the innovations that Charles Eames included, and which he hoped might catch on in other homes, was colored panels on the outside walls of the house. The panels were meant to be replaced whenever the homeowner wanted to freshen up the outside.

For innovators, color represents a challenge, the opportunity to address the world by changing its most basic vocabulary.

 **CHAPTER SEVEN**

Strains Never Heard Before

SOUND AND MUSIC

The angriest editorial ever seen in a New York newspaper may have been the one that ran in the *Times* on August 19, 1884. The subject was music and the rhetoric was caustic. "Men," it declared, "are no better than the instruments they play." It reiterated the point by putting words in the mouth of an imaginary criminal: "Let me make the instruments of a people and I care not who runs their Sunday schools." According to the *Times'* version of history, Spain had lost its dignity, along with its standing as a world power, after the guitar caught on there. A similar fate awaited the United States, but through a different scourge.

"Playing the banjo rapidly obliterates all sense of the distinction between truth and falsehood," the paper explained.

The player knows that he is merely making noises on an instrument, and will even sometimes call himself a musician. He soon loses the power to distinguish between a musical instrument and an instrument of noise, and from believing that music and noise are identical, he easily comes to believe that truth and falsehood are essentially the same.

Further on, the editorial left all such careful reasoning behind. "That men should commonly be visited with sudden death while playing the banjo is more than we have any right to hope," it sighed.

Admirably unrestrained, if slightly pathological, the editorial was based on a kernel of truth. People are indeed no better (or worse) than the instruments they play. The sounds they require, the noise they want, music does fill the mind with a second way of thinking and the heart, perchance, with a different way of feeling. For that reason, practically everyone likes some noise—that is to say, some style or genre of music—and dislikes others. In the first place, there is the instrument, and after that, the song.

The invention of an instrument is quite separate from the composition of music. An instrument has not the soul of music. Regarded without sentiment, it is nothing more than a soundmaker. An instrument has for its competition the neutral of silence (or ambient, background noise). If it makes an impressive sound, it improves upon the silence, according to the listener. If it makes an aggravating sound, silence is preferred. That is the arena in which musical instruments are introduced: if it makes a good sound, then music will, without fail, find its way into the instrument.

The banjo excited raw opinion in the mid-1880s because it carried something new into every note: an irrefutable sense of energy. It was a slap in the face to the more genteel form of parlor music and it instigated a revolution in the American mainstream, where it had been embraced as the latest fad. The fad may be long gone, but the revolution it fostered continues to this day.

As an invention, the banjo was introduced in its final form in about 1840. It had its roots, however, in ideas borrowed from another culture. Just exactly which culture it was has been hard to pinpoint, but the rudiments of the instrument came from Africa. The musicologist Michael T. Coolen surmised that Africans from the Senegambia region of western Africa brought a plucked lute called the xalam (pronounced *kalam*) when they were taken to America as slaves. The xalam was a hollowed gourd covered on one side by a hide, with an arm attached at one end to hold three or four strings across the body of the instrument. It was not materially different from plucked lutes used in various cultures around the world, though in many Senegambian tribes, the use of the xalam in ensembles had reached a particularly sophisticated level.

Members of the Senegambian Wolof tribe, who were brought to the New World in large numbers in the early eighteenth century, had a long tradition with the xalam in many forms. However, throughout the colonies and in the West Indies as well, slaves were forbidden from using their own ancestral instruments, lest they be used to spread messages in code. Drums, in particular, were outlawed. When Wolofs were confronted and asked about the stringed instrument that was growing so popular on plantations, they seemed to have replied that it was not theirs and not African at all, but European, using the word from their language for a non-Wolof stringed instrument: *banshaw.* Only in that way could they keep their music.

The banshaw was known by many names, including *banjer, bangil, bangy,* and *banza. Banjo,* the name that caught on, is more fetching than any of those, though even it is not as beguiling as some of the names that didn't stick: *strum-strum,* for example, and *merrywang.* Fashioned typically of a calabash gourd, which had the benefit of a stalk protruding from one end, the banjo was popular on many plantations. An Englishman who lived for a time in Maryland and Virginia commented on slaves he encountered who were "awakened and alive at the sound of the banjer." African Americans were not the only ones fascinated by the new sound of the banjo—what some people called

The banjo was introduced in its final form in about 1840. This five-string fretless banjo was made by William Boucher Jr., Baltimore, Maryland, 1846.

William Sidney Mount

Micah Hawkins ran a grocery store in New York in the early 1800s, a rather unique establishment, with a piano constructed into the front counter. Hawkins liked nothing more than to play songs for his customers—despite the fact that they would insist on interrupting every so often in order to buy food. Hawkins taught his nephew, William Sidney Mount, to love music, too, although Mount ultimately focused his life around a busy career in painting.

For recreation, William Mount enjoyed two hobbies: designing small boats and playing the violin. The two came together in 1852 when he designed a new kind of violin, which looked, in truth, strangely like a boat. Mount gave his invention a romantic name, the "Cradle of Harmony," and received a patent on it. The earliest version was straight-sided, without the pinched waist of standard violins, though it did widen through the body, starting from the neck to the base. Later editions were more conventional in appearance. In any case, the major distinction was in the back. Where standard Italian violins are either slightly convex or flat, the Cradle of Harmony was concave, meaning that the back curved slightly inward. (A marble would roll around and stay on the back of a Cradle of Harmony.)

The effect musically was a noticeably rich tone. Acoustically, it was a dramatically amplified sound. William Mount liked that. Most violinists played in drawing rooms and concert halls; Mount played regularly at dances. And he was something of a hard rocker, for his time, writing to his brother in reference to playing any violin: "Take out your old box and go at it, pell mell. . . . In shifting, slide your fingers up and down. You know what I mean."

Mount displayed his Cradle of Harmony at New York's Crystal Palace Exhibition. "This invention seems to demand more than ordinary attention," raved a critic at the show. "It is remarkable for extreme simplicity." Mount's nephew, a carriagemaker by trade, produced one of the three examples known to have been made. Mount left it at that. He was no businessman, just a part-time fiddler who wanted to be heard once in a while.

the "dismal monotony" of its notes and others praised as "wild notes of melody." A small number of Europeans and white Americans were drawn to the instrument, too, in the 1700s.

Sometime between 1790 and 1840, the modern banjo was invented. The earliest example is one originally owned by Joel Walker Sweeney of Virginia, constructed for his niece. That artifact, combined with Sweeney's promotion of banjo music, has led to the common acknowledgment of Sweeney as the inventor. In truth, the modern banjo was the work of many inventors, preponderantly African American slaves, it can be assumed. Their contributions are not lessened by the fact that their names may never be known.

A fifth string, adding a bass line, was one hallmark of the fully realized banjo. The fifth string was almost certainly invented by a slave since it was in sporadic use on plantations early in the 1800s. Another modernized feature lay with the shape of the body. Rather than a lopsided gourd, the new body was perfectly round, allowing for the inclusion of another innovation—clamps that could be used to tighten the hide across the body. That improvement may have been inspired by another endeavor entirely. As cheese factories grew in size and output in the 1820s, they began to ship cheese in small wooden barrels that could be sliced at one end—like the end of a cheese log—to make a body for a banjo. The addition of frets along the neck was probably a contribution from someone familiar with European instruments such as the mandolin or guitar.

A traditional jazz band—of which the banjo was an integral part—plays at a party in New Orleans in 2005.

The combination of experiences that produced the modern banjo only adds to its place as an American icon. The instrument itself may have its roots in other cultures, but the sound it makes is quintessentially American. Along the way, however, it became a painful symbol for its primary inventors.

The banjo was adopted by many amateur musicians in free society (that is, whites and freed slaves) who played classical works in ensemble. It was much more popular, though, as a prop in the minstrel shows that borrowed the basics of the music developed by African Americans and combined it with parody of their lives. Before long, the banjo was associated with the hapless figures depicted by the minstrels, and for that reason many African Americans steered clear of the instrument and the stereotype it purveyed. The stigma faded by the early twentieth century when the banjo became integral to the Dixieland style of jazz, pioneered by African Americans.

In the meantime, others were picking away at banjos, doggedly trying to master the combination of rhythm and melody. And each and every one of them was annoying the *New York Times*. The highest praise for the banjo is contained in the paper's scorn. "The banjo is the offspring of a dissolute guitar and a shameless drum," it spat. "It is simply an instrument of noise." But that's exactly the point. The banjo gave vent to intense energy and improvisation at a time when neither was part of mainstream music. It was the banjo that gave "wild notes" to popular music and has let every generation since believe that it was the first to crank up the energy.

In terms of cranking up the sound and adding decibels to a piece of music, Joshua C. Stoddard was the master, waking the world up with a jolt on July 4, 1855, when he demonstrated his steam calliope on the streets of Worcester, Massachusetts. As far as twelve miles away, people suddenly looked up in farm fields and back kitchens and wondered why they were hearing the strains of "Rosalie" coming from the direction of Worcester. Anyone right next to the calliope that day was trying hard just to remain upright in the sudden gale-force storm of loud music.

Stoddard's invention consisted of a chest about six feet by four feet in dimension that fed steam into an array of eight valves on the top. The valves were opened temporarily by a piston rod mechanism that turned underneath the array and could be programmed in advance, in the manner of a music box. Each valve was connected to a steam whistle capable of making a different note; the whistles also responded to stimuli from the piston rods, rising or lowering to effect a sharp or a flat.

The reliance on the steam whistle was no coincidence. As a boy in Vermont, Stoddard had listened to steam whistles on passing trains. He heard music in them. Still fascinated much later in life, he resolved to build a fully melodic instrument based on the same concept. With lofty intentions, he named his invention the calliope, after the ancient Greek Muse of poetry. A reporter present at the demonstration in 1855 considered it epoch-making. "This invention," wrote the correspondent, "will alter the tone of public demonstration on important occasions very essentially. . . . On our nation's anniversary we shall hear,—instead of the brutal roar of cannon—some spirited ode with a 'national air.'" The fact that the steam whistles were so very loud inspired Stoddard's own marketing plan: he thought he would sell them

Man playing a steam calliope on the levee in Cincinnati, Ohio.

to churches, to replace mere bells. "It is not necessary for us to show in how many ways this new wonder may be made delightful," gushed the newspaper correspondent who had seen the calliope, and heard it, "but we leave it to the imaginative mind to conceive of its application and its harmonious beauty."

The churches weren't quite so impressed; they all turned Stoddard down. The more he promised that it could be heard all over the countryside, the more the churches disdained it.

Steamboats were not as demure. A ship called the *Glen Cove* operated out of New York City—usually with only a couple of passengers onboard. As a final desperate move to draw attention, the owners installed a calliope and played a tune whenever it approached a dock. Business boomed. The calliope could be regarded as an early form of broadcasting, imparting an immediacy that no printed matter could match. Many steamboats adopted them, and when the vessels approached, people ten miles inland knew it. Early on, a keyboard had replaced the piston mechanism, so any pianist could play the calliope. Not many, however, would want to. The calliope was so hot that the keys had to be made of brass, lest they burn. The same provision couldn't be made for the hands of the player—who was typically known as the "professor"—onboard ship. Even as his fingers were singed on the hot brass, he had to dodge blasts of steam from the whistles. Sitting atop the volcano, the professor was also under assault by the full force of the sound. But it was worth the duress, as the calliope gave a player what every virtuoso covets: the world for an audience.

According to an 1859 report in the London *News,* a calliope was installed on the coast of Nova Scotia to communicate with passing ships;

A steamboat called the *Glen Cove*, which operated out of New York City, had a steam calliope onboard to attract passengers.

over water, the sound could be heard at a distance of twenty-five miles. Armies were said to be considering the use of calliopes in battle, to signal new orders.

Circuses were no less reticent about attracting attention, and they quickly adopted a wagon-size calliope. It joined the traditional parade that announced the arrival of the circus in town, typically taking up the rear. Children who found circuses irresistible answered the calliope like a clarion call, dropping whatever they were doing to follow its song.

In 1905, an inventor named Joseph Uri renewed the popularity of the calliope with a version driven by a gasoline or electric motor rather than steam, and with compressed air as the medium of

Wagon-size steam calliope from a circus.

the music. His "calliaphone" was more cooperative than the old steam dragons; it had a volume control and could be played at less than foghorn levels. It was the steam calliope that reached into the heart, though, with its audacious, unyielding tower of melodious sound. In 1949, when Harry Truman was sworn into office for his second term as president, with Alben Barkley as his vice president, the organizers of the inaugural parade received an unusual request. The owners of a steam calliope from Barkley's home state of Kentucky asked if they could bring their machine. It was given the place of honor for a calliope: at the rear of the parade. Army battalions, marching bands, floats, and an airborne parade of intercontinental bombers preceded it in a procession a mile-and-a-quarter long, but the calliope came through at the very end. Following behind it was a gaggle of quite elderly men, about a dozen of them, stepping lively and almost dancing. They'd heard the sound of the calliope and answered its call, doing what they'd learned to do a long, long time before—all in a carefree spell.

• • •

The professors who played the steam calliopes on the steamboats or in the circus were prey to an occupational hazard (aside from callused fingertips and lobster-red faces): they very often lost their hearing from exposure to so much noise.

Inventors in the nineteenth century had energetically attacked the problem of restoring the ability to hear, though to be more accurate, most of the creative work addressed a peripheral problem: inducing people who were hard of hearing to use their ear trumpets. The ear trumpet, an exaggerated version of the hand cupped over the ear, had been in use for centuries. Shaped like a giant funnel, it gathered sound waves from the air and concentrated them into the ear. It also made people feel conspicuous and tended to make them embarrassed. Small boys insisted on mistaking the ear trumpet for a cornet, and when a deaf person took one out to use it, they delighted in demanding a song. Even King Edward VII of Great Britain, who was not known for his reticence in many areas, kept his deafness to himself, refusing to be seen with any such apparatus. The only people who actually liked the ear trumpet were writers of low comedy, who learned to look to them for easy laughs.

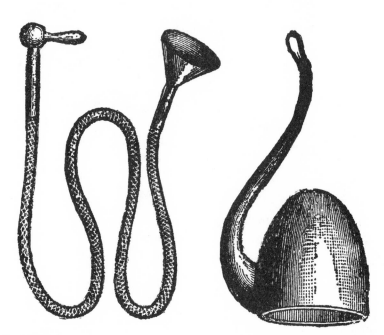

Ear trumpets.

Taking the problem of the hilarious ear trumpet seriously, a cadre of inventors came to the rescue. They made the problem no better—but a great deal funnier. A St. Louis inventor disguised the ear trumpet as an umbrella. Out in public and wishing to have a conversation, a man had only to turn his umbrella around and put the point in his ear. "He has thus an efficient ear trumpet," noted a reporter who couldn't resist spoofing the invention, "without exciting the slightest suspicion that he is deaf."

Spectators will merely notice that he is holding an umbrella to his ear, and will suppose that he is an eccentric person—a philosopher, for instance—who is listening to remarks of an unusually profound character. When two umbrellas are used even the deafest of men can hear. In this case the deaf man uses one umbrella as an ear trumpet and his companion uses the other as a speaking trumpet. A conversational duet on two umbrellas can thus be readily carried on without attracting the disagreeable attention that an ordinary ear trumpet always attracts.

A more ambitious approach was taken by Dr. Samuel Sexton of New York, who made successful experiments in transmitting sound waves to the ear through the bones of the skull.

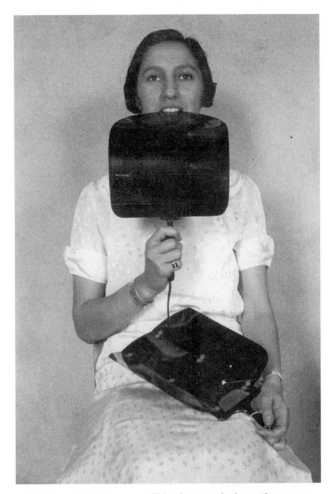

This photograph shows the Rhodes Audiophone. Sound was gathered through the fan area, then traveled via the upper teeth to the inner ear by bone conduction.

His invention, called the otacoustic fan, was introduced in 1881. It employed a fairly standard fan of the lacquered Japanese type then in vogue. The sound waves collected by the fan traveled along a cord to a plate held firmly but gently against the teeth. Sexton's patients reported that the device worked quite well, but its drawback was its range. While the ear trumpet conducted sound from a distance of twelve feet, the otacoustic fan was limited to three feet.

Alexander Graham Bell was as committed as anyone to inventing a means of assisting the deaf, a pursuit that ultimately inspired his work on the telephone. Yet it was an Alabama-born electrical engineer who perfected the first practical hearing aid. Miller Reese Hutchison was an inventor at heart. "First of all, I have seen a need," he explained of his best work. "Then I have set to work to fill that need by applying the well-known laws of physics. Nothing I have done has been creative." Without being creative, Hutchison would eventually become one of the most prolific inventors of his time. His output ranged from a device to reduce the chance of carbon monoxide poisoning from automobile emissions to a special film that could be magnified to forty-eight times its original size, thus making possible the spy camera.

Hutchison had been an athletic youth, a bicycle champion, show rider, and swimmer. He later credited his ability to work ninety hours in a typical week to his robust approach to exercise. Later in life, he worked a full day as a private investor in his Wall Street office, returned home to New Jersey for dinner, and then worked until 1:30 a.m. in his laboratory, churning out inventions at a steady pace. The lack of sleep suited Hutchison, as it did Thomas Edison, with whom he worked in the 1910s. Hutchison was known to be a relaxed, genial man, and very fond of humor in his conversations. He developed a wide circle of friends, including Mark Twain. As an inventor, his favorite pursuit was acoustics—a technical field by any measure, but one that had the lingering aura of a fairy tale for Miller Hutchison.

In 1899, as a twenty-three-year-old graduate of Alabama Polytechnic Institute, Hutchison was in New York City, developing a hearing aid—one based not on ear trumpets or even umbrellas, but on electricity. Other inventors had tried the same route, but the resulting sound was murky at best. Hutchison investigated all of the possibilities and ultimately employed a carbon-based transmitter, or microphone, patented by Thomas Edison thirteen years before. He sealed it in rubber, with a mixture of gases that improved the quality of the relay. Once Hutchison was able to achieve clear results in the conversational range of tones, he named his invention the Acousticon. It consisted of a tabletop box containing the microphone, battery, and transmitter, with wires carrying the sound, amplified as needed, to a headset.

Miller Reese Hutchison, c. 1925. Hutchison was a prolific inventor who was born in Alabama and lived in New Jersey.

"I had a friend," he later recalled, "who was a deaf-mute. The acousticon was the result of love for him and a desire to make him hear. I also hoped that after he could hear, he could learn to speak. But he never did. He seemed to be content with hearing." After serving with the U.S. government in the Spanish-American War, Hutchison promoted the Acousticon in earnest, giving demonstrations in New York City. "The most hopeless persons in the New York Institution for the Deaf and Dumb," noted someone who attended a well-scrutinized demonstration there, "some who had never heard a sound in all their lives, put the little instrument to the ears and listened to Sousa's marches, and one of them, a boy born deaf, danced to a twostep, the first music he had ever heard."

The Acousticon, a hearing aid invented by Miller Reese Hutchison.

As Hutchison pointed out, the invention could restore hearing for about 55 percent of those regarded as deaf; it helped 40 percent to some degree, and could do little for the remaining 5 percent. By 1901–2, the apparatus had been reduced in size such that the transmitter could be worn on the clothing and the battery hidden under a belt or lapel.

One day in 1902, a refined Englishwoman unexpectedly appeared at one of Hutchison's demonstrations. She was furtive in manner and didn't deign to introduce herself to Hutchison. Her official title was Consuelo, Dowager Duchess of Manchester. Unbeknownst to anyone else, she had been sent on her mission by Queen Alexandra, who had been hard of hearing most of her life. Her husband, King Edward VII, was already quite deaf, and so the condition represented a serious family concern. When the queen received word regarding the promise of the Acousticon, she sent Consuelo to investigate. So it was that Hutchison later received a request from one of the queen's ladies-in-waiting, asking him to travel to London and meet with "a very prominent patient." Hutchison suspected, correctly, that the patient was none other than the queen and he made sure to catch an early liner for England. After preliminary tests involving others, he let the queen try on the earpiece. He was nervous, but that was nothing. Consuelo, the Dowager Duchess, was downright numb. If the queen detected no improvement, if she

Queen Alexandra, wife of King Edward VII, had been hard of hearing most of her life.

received a shock from the battery, or if she just plain didn't like it, Hutchison could go home. The Dowager Duchess had to remain in a much icier England.

"The Queen put on the receiver," Hutchison later recalled, "and earpiece, and I addressed various sentences to her which contained things which I felt she would not expect. She repeated all of them correctly. Her gratification at the success of the device was marked." After spending two months at Buckingham Palace helping the queen adjust to the Acousticon, Hutchison received a gold medal from the royal couple "for scientific investigation and invention" and went home to America, where the Acousticon was rarely mentioned without the queen's name cropping up as a satisfied customer.

"Very little has really been learned about sound," Hutchison observed twenty-five years later. "Architects continue to erect buildings in which sound is carried poorly. A great deal of my time has been spent correcting defects in acoustics. Sometimes only a thicker wall somewhere, another opening or a partition, is required." Sometimes, though, Hutchison found that subtlety didn't count as much as brute power.

After the success of the hearing aid, Hutchison splurged on a fancy car and was driving it one foggy night through Newark, New Jersey. Suddenly, a man darted into the road. Hutchison was certain that the car was going to run him over. He slammed on the brakes and honked the horn. Fortunately, the brakes worked better than the horn. The man was spared, but Hutchison was incensed that in the name of elegance, the car's horn was a gentle, melodious tinkle. "Then and there," he recalled, "I decided that automobiles should have a horn that startled, shocked and repelled instantly." He invented the Klaxon, a horn that relied on electricity to vibrate a metal diaphragm, emitting a sound that was shrill yet guttural, abrupt yet unending, ugly yet lifesaving. It was Hutchison who gave the "owwooga" call to early motoring. Car companies adopted the Klaxon or copied it, adding to the cacophony of the urban traffic jam and leading Mark Twain to tell Hutchison, "You invented the Klaxon horn to make people deaf, so they'd have to use your acoustic device in order to make them hear again."

In the 1920s, the only sound considered more obnoxious than a Klaxon horn—which was supposed to be obnoxious—was the ukelele, which was supposed to be cute. The miniature, four-string guitar made notes into "plings" in the manner of a toy xylophone, but it was easy to play and had an insouciance appealing to its youthful virtuosos. In fact, the ukelele replaced the banjo as the favorite instrument of the college campus, in part because it was simpler to learn and in part, perhaps, because the banjo was rising to new standards of musical style through its popularity in jazz and even mountain music. A person could be a bad banjo player: that wasn't noticeably true of the ukelele.

Many of those who played the ukelele, hoping it evoked the ocean breezes and swaying palms of its native Hawaii, assumed that the instrument was native to the islands; that is, that Hawaiians had developed it in ancient times. To a true Hawaiian, though, the ukelele was, to use the Wolof term, a "banshaw"—an unfamiliar instrument. The inventor of the ukelele was Manuel Nunes, who had been born on Madeira, an island belonging to Portugal. Moving to Hawaii in 1878, he found that musical instruments were scarce and so he constructed his own little guitar, using a cigar box for the body. He tuned it in a simple key and found that it made a light, distinctive sound. Tourists took an avid interest in it, and Nunes found a career as a ukulele maker, an art that he passed on to his family.

In 1922, Nunes died at the age of eighty, a hero in some quarters. He had accomplished the dream of offering a new sound, a way to release the noise playing inside of people's heads. The ukelele, in that sense, was not merely a construction of wood and strings; it was a language. Not everyone was grateful. "There are ever so many people who might wish," offered one eulogy to Nunes, "that he could have taken the ukelele with him when he passed into the other world."

In 1947, Carleen Maley Hutchins was a former science teacher living with her husband and newborn son in New York. Born in 1911, she had grown up in Montclair, New Jersey, where her mother had taken pains to give her an upbringing free of constrictions. In junior high school, for example, when Carleen wanted to take wood shop rather than home economics, her mother encouraged her. The school had no choice but to comply. Carleen later graduated from Cornell University, a young woman with a noticeably direct manner but a friendly disposition.

As a housewife in the late 1940s, Hutchins decided on something of a lark—she took up the viola. She bought a secondhand instrument and started practicing. Having learned enough to know that what she owned was a very poor excuse for a viola, she announced to her friends that she wanted a new one and intended to build it herself. One of her friends scoffed and promised that if Hutchins could build a viola, she'd eat her hat. Two years later, she was cutting into a cake shaped like a hat.

Hutchins brought a combination of science and musicology to her new pursuit: building instruments in the violin family. After studying with a luthier (violin maker) in New York City, she was fully qualified to build instruments, but to study them at the level she intended, she was happy to admit that she was still in need of help. Through another friend, Hutchins met Frederick A. Saunders, the retired chairman of the Physics Department at Harvard University. An amateur violinist,

Saunders wanted to devote his retirement to acoustical studies of the violin. The two formed an alliance, with Hutchins crafting instruments specifically for experimentation. The goal was measurable analysis of the sound produced by a violin.

Working with Saunders and others, Hutchins learned to approach violin making as a science, reducing the mysteries surrounding the instrument. A superb violin could not be mass-produced, but it could be understood according to the laws of physics. "It is possible," she commented in the early 1990s, "for violin makers today, using technical information that's been developed over the last thirty years, to make fine violins every time. There is no reason to pay millions of dollars to get a good instrument."

By the late 1950s, Hutchins was regarded as one of the world's foremost authorities on the violin. She could have continued making instruments according to the standards she had developed, but instead she set off with a new goal. The challenge was suggested by a musicologist with a far-fetched idea, something never attempted before: a set of violins created and matched to play the full range of the musical scale. The violin octet, as it was called, was to be capable of playing a full symphony, replacing every other string instrument in the orchestra. To accomplish the feat, Hutchins would have to create eight new instruments, most of them invented according to her knowledge of acoustics and musical dynamics.

The eight instruments were the tiny treble violin (about three-quarters the size of a standard instrument), the soprano violin, the mezzo violin, the alto violin, the tenor violin, the baritone violin, the small bass violin, and the contrabass violin (about six feet in length).

The first of Hutchins' violin octets made its debut in 1965. One critic responded by exclaiming, "A major step toward renovating the string family for the first time in 200 years has been taken—and bravo!" Eventually, Hutchins completed seven octets. Most are housed in museums around the world, but one, in Los Angeles, is used in a regular series of concerts by a group calling itself the Hutchins Consort.

In 2007, at the age of ninety-six, Hutchins was still regarded as a treasure in the world of instrument makers, an innovator and inventor in the settled world of violin making. She had not only given forth a new sound through the octet, but also accomplished something even more rare. She coaxed a new sound out of an instrument that had been thought to be thoroughly explored. It was tantamount to finding a new island where everyone else thought there was only water.

As the *Times* editorialist had scoffed, people as a rule are no better than the instruments they play. If that is so, then the Hutchins octet gave Americans reason to be rather contented with their lot.

 **CHAPTER EIGHT**

The Irresistible Invention

FOOD AND THE TASTE OF SOMETHING NEW

More than six thousand people made a pilgrimage to a working farm in Santa Rosa, California, during the year 1904, uninvited and, if the truth be known, not particularly welcome.

Having traveled from all over the world, visitors weren't likely to be overwhelmed by the first view that the place had to offer. The front consisted of a short walkway, lined with flower boxes in the California style, leading to a simple cottage. The property, covering a scant eight acres, wasn't by any means the biggest farm in the state. And beyond shovels and shears, it boasted little in the way of equipment. In the popular estimation, though, Luther Burbank's farm was the most productive and advanced in the entire country, if not the world. The surroundings may well have been old-fashioned, but that was all right by the proprietor. It was the plants that were state-of-the-art.

Luther Burbank made a life's work of inventing plants. Inspired by two of Charles Darwin's books, *The Variation of Animals and Plants under Cultivation* and *The Effects of Cross and Self-Fertilisation in the Vegetable Kingdom*, he turned out new varieties of corn, plums, potatoes, peas, and hundreds of other foodstuffs almost continuously from about 1880 until his death in 1926. Improving yields along with marketability, he came to be regarded as the pioneer of plant breeders, a living example of the constant need for innovation in the effort to keep the population fed—and beyond that, well fed.

Luther Burbank.

Taste and eating reflect a decidedly personal sphere, a unique overlap of the worlds of health and art, science and emotion. That same sphere presents an irresistible opportunity for the inventor to simplify a complex process, that of bringing food from the source to the table, three times a day, and with nearly infinite choice for the diner. With so many points of discretion along the way, the food industry draws inventors at every level of ambition, from home cooks with a new idea to scientists such as Luther Burbank who change the course of nations.

Burbank may have been the most famous, but he wasn't the first of the plant inventors in the United States. In 1837, Charles Hovey, a nurseryman in Cambridge, Massachusetts, decided to brave the rocky route of creating a hybrid. Formally defined in 1761, hybridization consisted of cross-breeding two specific plants in hopes of retaining the most desirable attributes of each in the offspring. Depending on the type of plant, it sometimes required hand pollination. The hybrid process could be frustrating—as when the resulting plant reached up toward the sky, full of hope and the very worst attributes of each of its parent plants. Just as troubling, a hybrid plant was often sterile. Nonetheless, hybridization represented just the kind of bold stroke that Charles Hovey hoped would startle American horticulture out of what he regarded as a complacent slumber. Hovey's argument was that American agriculture was hobbled by nothing less than its own political history.

Outrage of some sort is at the base of most human accomplishment and certainly of invention in food as well. Hovey couldn't understand why the country that had governed America at its colonial stage should be the mother country in all matters forever. "As yet," Hovey complained, "the plants of nearly all the kinds in cultivation have been introduced from the English gardens, and are not suited to the severity of our climate."

His argument might be dismissed with a shrug, but it would be won with a brand-new plant to prove the point. "Mr. Hovey," explained a friend, "resolved to produce an American strawberry." With no particular scientific training, Hovey set out to cross-breed six existing types in order to invent the best possible strawberry for American conditions. He succeeded brilliantly with the "Hovey strawberry" that resulted. Yet, despite his reputation as a meticulous horticulturist, Hovey later had to admit that he had unfortunately misplaced his notes on his experiment. He never could remember which plant he had crossed with which to produce his famous strawberry, and so, as with any newly landed American, the new berry could only be judged by its future, not its ancestry. The first documented American hybrid plant, the Hovey strawberry gave flavorful berries that were very large, at least by the standards of the nineteenth century. Even more important, it became the basis for most subsequent American varieties. Hovey never developed another plant, turning to magazine work afterward. But he had made his point.

Robert Nelson, a horticulturist from Denmark, moved to Georgia in 1843 and had the distinction of being the first to see it for what it was: the peach state. Before he arrived in 1843, peaches were a sideline for growers, with yields that were unpredictable and fruit that was quick to rot. Nelson was adamant that local farmers take peaches more seriously, and he was convinced that a tree could be invented that would thrive in the Georgia soil. He established a nursery in Macon, Georgia, bringing to it the latest breeding techniques from his studies in Europe. Inventing a tree that takes fifteen years to mature could require a lifetime or two, allowing for mistakes. Nelson depended in part on grafting: inculcating a branch or bud from one tree into another. Convincing the first tree to accept a branch from another takes the skill of a surgeon and the care of an expert nurse, but it allows for propagation of a tree with the best characteristics of different species. Moreover, Nelson could produce plantable trees in the course of a season or two, rather than a couple of decades. By grafting native types with ones shipped from other regions, Nelson invented a reliable new type of peach tree, suited to Georgia and its neighboring states. He made one small mistake, though—he didn't give his new type of peach tree a name.

"Depend upon it," said a contemporary, Jarvis Van Buren, who specialized in apples, "a name is as useful to a fruit as it is to a man. It will not make its way in the world without a good one." Even in anonymity, Nelson's peach tree was a sensation. It certainly caught the attention of Georgia farmers, who had previously sold their peaches for twenty-five cents a bushel in New York markets.

Nelson sent a load of his peaches north and received fifty cents a peach. In fact, "Fifty Cents a" might have been the best name for the new peach, so often was that mantra repeated in Georgia, as farmers scrambled to buy and plant the new type of tree and receive their "fifty cents a peach." By the time the Civil War broke out in 1861, Northerners were clamoring to buy sweet, juicy Georgia peaches. With the war, though, that market vanished. Worse, many thriving orchards were decimated during the fighting and its aftermath, with valuable trees being chopped down for fuel during the dark days of 1864–65. It took yet another generation to bring the peach back to blossom, on the descendants of the trees Robert Nelson had invented by beginning with grafting.

In Concord, Massachusetts, Ephraim Wales Bull used the more basic process of selection to develop the Concord grape in the 1840s. As a workman in Boston, Bull harbored a fascination with grape growing, and a frustration with the fact that European grapes grew to no more than a puny size in his corner of North America. On a farm he owned between the towns of Lexington and Concord, he planted tens of thousands of vines, searching through them, year in and year out, for a hardy plant with robust grapes. One year, Bull noticed a wild labrusca grape plant growing at the edge of his vineyard. It looked healthier than all of his other plants put together.

The labrusca was the prevalent native grape of the eastern United States, but it had drawbacks, both in taste and in the haphazard "gypsy" way that it grew. Bull was intrigued with the one growing on his border. "I put these grapes into the ground, skins and all," Bull recalled. "I nursed these seedlings six years, and of the large number obtained, only one proved to be worth keeping." Bull selected the best of each generation

The first Concord grape vines, above, are seen growing on an arbor at Ephraim Wales Bull's farm in Concord, Massachusetts, in 1849. Bull, a metalworker by trade, cultivated the new variety as a hobby. Today, the nation produces some 672 million pounds of Concord grapes annually.

Roller mill.

and made new plantings until he arrived at the sweet, versatile Concord grape. He introduced it at a horticultural show in Boston, where it was received with a thunderclap of excitement. Bull tried to sell it, but before he could take charge, cuttings were being traded and mailed all over the country. The Concord seemed to be happy practically everywhere. Within a half dozen years, it was in cultivation throughout the Northeast and as far west as the Mississippi River. Bull, for his part, was not as astonished at the popularity of his plump grape in backyards and commercial fields as he was by how little money he'd made off the big success.

With western lands opening for broad cultivation after the Civil War, the need for productive seeds was acute. Not only were vast tracts being newly planted, but invention in farm implements was the pride of the age, allowing for processing of vegetables and grains that were once thought unmanageable. Hard wheats were one example. While they had the inherent advantage of resisting droughts common to the plains, they were notoriously reluctant to part with their chaff. The invention of the automated roller mill in Minneapolis in 1878 opened the market for new strains of hard wheats and changed the fortunes of the northern plains. The federal government sponsored research and innovation through programs considered massive at the time. Land-grant colleges typically emphasized agricultural research, but more pointedly, agricultural experiment stations launched by the Hatch Act of 1887 gave invention in plant research an official place in government. With dozens of such stations in operation by the 1890s, specialized new plants were produced in a steady stream.

And yet the number of people visiting the average agricultural substation in 1904 was probably somewhat less than the six thousand heading for the Burbank farm that year. The grand total at a particularly popular station might be about six. The draw at Burbank's farm was in part the dazzle of celebrity. Luther Burbank has to be credited with taking one of the least understood callings—plant invention, which is, from one point of view, exactly as exciting as watching grass grow—and painting it with the adventure he knew from his own experience.

There was no money to speak of in developing new plants. Patent protection wasn't available until 1930, and seed companies were unceasingly efficient in appropriating popular strains. Ephraim Wales Bull was one of the few plant inventors of the time who went into his research frankly hoping to make money. His epitaph reflects the folly in that, especially in his era. It read: "He sowed, others reaped." Burbank had no such illusions about money. He did, however, understand publicity and nurtured his own image, as he did his other seedlings, until he was famous throughout the land as "the Wizard of Horticulture" or "Wizard" Burbank.

The Wizard had been born and raised in Massachusetts. He was the kind of boy who had a cactus for a pet and he liked to carry it around the house for company. Even before that, when he was a toddler, his parents and eleven older brothers and sisters knew how to stop him from crying: "A blossom," his sister wrote, "placed in the baby's hands would always stay his tears." As a teenager, Burbank had vague ideas about studying medicine, but he never strayed far from his first love; he would

The invention of the automated roller mill in Minneapolis in 1878 opened the market for new strains of hard wheats, which had the inherent advantage of resisting droughts common to the plains.

linger in farm fields just to look at the plants. On the way to school each day, he passed a field of potatoes and took a special interest in them because they were of a new variety called Early Rose. Descended from South American wild potatoes, the Early Rose was the product of cross-breeding, a process that fascinated Burbank. As he perused the field one day, he noticed a seed pod—a rarity on any potato plant, but a particular curiosity on an Early Rose, which produced so few of them.

Burbank picked the pod when it was mature, counted twenty-two seeds inside, and carefully planted them. Perhaps because the Early Rose was still a young breed, the seeds produced twenty-two very different potato plants. Burbank recognized that one of them bore a superior potato, rounded and fleshy, and he cultivated it through further generations into a new variety.

In the meantime, Burbank's uncle secured a job for him in the Ames Manufacturing Company's factory in Worcester. The young man had long been interested in steam engines, and his parents thought he would naturally become a mechanic. The job at Ames involved turning wooden parts for plows, and the pay was fifty cents a day. Burbank leapt at the job and then realized that his room and board in Worcester was also fifty cents a day. With a six-day workweek and a seven-day life, he realized that he was losing money. "As this arrangement did not appeal to my business instincts," Burbank recalled, "I induced my uncle to grant me the privilege of working by the piece instead of by the day." He was soon earning a dollar a day. Then he started thinking:

> I had not been long at the work before the knack at contriving things mechanical came to my aid. I conceived an improvement in the turning lathe that would enable me, I thought, to perform the work much more expeditiously. The invention proved a success, and with its aid I was enabled to earn as much as sixteen dollars a day.

Burbank longed to turn his inventive mind to plants, his earliest fascination. In 1873, he sold the potato plant that he'd originated to a local businessman for $125. The purchaser named it the "Burbank potato," and its fame spread quickly. Burbank's supporters later claimed the variety quashed the Irish Potato Famine, though those claims were not substantiated. By the end of the twentieth century, the Burbank did comprise 60 percent of the U.S. potato crop, 91 percent of that in Idaho.

The Burbank potato resulted more from chance, a well-educated guess, than from horticultural planning. But beginner's luck is the most intoxicating of all, and the experience left Burbank wanting to do it again. Within weeks of receiving payment for the potato plant, he was on his way to California, where two of his brothers already lived. Luther Burbank set up shop as a nurseryman, specializing in the development of new varieties of fruits, vegetables, and flowers. In his own view, his choice of a career was not far from his parents' dream for him: the good Yankee life of making and running practical machinery. Inventing plants demanded the same creativity and the same stubborn desire to make some aspect of a hard life easier. His love of plants took him away to California and his eight acres of careful plantings there, but his Yankee ingenuity remained intact. Guided by practical instincts inherited from his parents, as he reflected, "and the love of mechanics that was only second to my love of nature, the inventive propensities that had found earlier vent in the manufacture of steam engines and new turning devices were to be applied to the plastic material of the living plant. Just where it all might lead no one could say."

At first, it led Burbank to employment as a common laborer—when he could find a job. At one work camp, he was told that he could have a job if he brought a special kind of axe, so he went to a store and spent his last few dollars to buy one. By the time he returned with it, the job had been filled. For the better part of ten years, Burbank barely survived. He sometimes went hungry in order to keep the farm afloat, sacrificing his youth for the sake of the plants. It was not an unusual state for an inventor with new ideas: the sacrifice tests the intention. Eventually, Burbank began to see success, in terms of the propagation of his newly developed plants. The tribulations left him resentful, though, and the more his reputation grew, the more he pointed at the hollow years, almost blaming his thousands of newfound disciples for ignoring him then.

Burbank turned California's yellow poppies red. He recast the wild and weedy daisy into an exuberant garden flower, the Shasta daisy. He gave the world an early corn, a pitless plum, a spineless cactus, the white blackberry, the thornless raspberry, and enough other horticultural oxymorons to become something of a punch line for wags everywhere. They made a game of it, requesting that Burbank next invent the boneless haddock, an eggplant with an omelette attached, a rhubarb that grew inside of a pie crust, and nongrowing lawn grass.

Part of the Burbank mystique emanated from the almost absurdly wide array of plants that he invented from 1873 until his death in 1926. Other horticulturists concentrated on one strain for years, considering themselves fortunate if even a single important plant resulted. Burbank could juggle dozens of projects, some of them unraveling over the course of ten years or more, some taking only a season. "Wizard" Burbank was the subject of regular features in the newspapers and magazines, a celebrity inventor; he was as remote as the techniques he kept shrouded at Santa Rosa for many years, and as familiar as the everyday products he invented: daisies, plums, and peas. After the bumper crop of tourists in 1906, he closed the farm to visitors. He was more public than ever, though, allowing backers to operate a publishing venture to express his story as he wished it told. After that, he didn't grant quite so many interviews, and he even set a price for interviews: $10 per hour. All that did was garner more publicity and more people driving past the gate to see the man whose conversation was so valuable.

At the turn of the twentieth century, many of the finest hotels in the country were owned and operated by African Americans. Typically, the proprietors had progressed from jobs as waiters or cooks, as is often the case in the hospitality industry. Joseph Lee, who had been a steward for eleven years, worked his way into proprietorship of the Woodland Park Hotel in

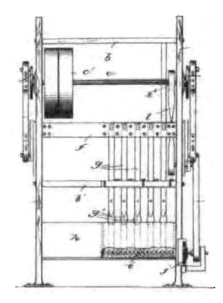

Top: Jospeh Lee's kneading machine of 1894 included a trough, marked H, in which ingredients were placed, and screwlike devices, marked I, where the mixture was kneaded into dough.

Bottom: Joseph Lee's Woodland Park Hotel.

Auburndale, Massachusetts. The writer William Dean Howells, known as a sharp critic, at least of literary works, was devoted to Lee and gave Woodland Park's restaurant enthusiastic reviews. Practically everyone in Lee's large following raved about his bread.

Lee had become a student of bread and bread making during his days as a steward. He noticed that the secret lay with the kneading, which had to be thorough and gentle. He recognized that a machine would make better dough than the average baker, but he never tried to replicate the actions of human hands. Instead, he took the leap crucial to many successful inventions and swept his mind clear of what he already knew—in his case, what he already knew about the mechanics of kneading. He thought only about the desired result and came up with a system of rotating arms that would mix the dough, even as it stretched and compressed it, by turns. Lee's machine worked beautifully, yet he didn't seek fame as an inventor, only as a restaurateur. Even while using the machine at the hotel, he kept it a secret until one of his patrons, one as devoted as Howells and even more brash, swept into the kitchen to see for himself how the bread was made. With that, Lee patented his bread-making machine. It didn't take bakers long to realize that liberation was at hand; they no longer had to stand at a board by the hour kneading. Lee went on to produce other inventions, but the basic principle of his bread-kneader is still in use in bakeries to this day.

One day, Jean Rosendahl looked up with an idea, having just noted, as everyone does, that spreading butter on corn on the cob and then seasoning it with salt and pepper is practically an impossible undertaking. In the first place, it requires three hands. The average person makes do with two, and both come away smeared with butter—which is more than can be said for the far side of the corn.

Rosendahl envisioned a solution. She wiped off her fingers one day in 1949 and drew a picture of a shallow dish, as long and narrow as an ear of corn. The idea was that melted butter would collect in the bottom of the dish, where it could be salted and peppered at will. An ear of corn, placed in the dish, would turn through it and come up uniformly seasoned. Rosendahl called her invention a "corn roller." She indicated notches for each end, by which to position the corn, and gave her sketch to a silversmith, who set to work making a set of custom-made corn rollers. As soon as they arrived, Rosendahl scheduled a dinner party featuring corn on the cob in order to test the roller under actual buttering conditions.

Jean Rosendahl was a Texan who had worked as a department store buyer before her marriage in 1934. Her husband was an inventor, too, and a celebrated figure in the world of lighter-than-air aviation. Charles E. Rosendahl invented three devices pertaining to the navigation of dirigibles—his enthusiasm for the huge airships never wavering despite the fact that he had been on board the U.S. Navy's *Shenandoah* on September 8, 1925, when it ripped apart over Ohio, killing fourteen of his crewmates. Charles Rosendahl retired as a rear admiral in 1945, laden with military honors, and he continued to work on potential inventions, including a design for a dirigible aircraft carrier. Unfortunately, his enthusiasm for airships was not matched in many quarters and his inventions were obsolete even before they left his drawing board. Jean Rosendahl was more practical in her career as an inventor—everyone, after all, likes corn on the cob.

The dinner party was an unqualified success, except for the moment when the admiral lost his grip on a piece of corn and let it crash into the dish. Butter rained all over the table. Perhaps because he was no longer an active-duty admiral, nobody blamed the dish. Not long after the party, Jean Rosendahl applied for a patent for her "Serving Dish for Corn on the Cob" and put it on the market, in ceramic form with a maize motif. Within a year, corn rollers were sitting on picnic tables all over the country. The inventor was gratified—and appalled, because hardly any of the companies manufacturing corn rollers were paying her royalties. Coming from a fighting household, she sued—and won.

"It wasn't a matter of money," Rosendahl said in an interview at her estate in Toms River, New Jersey. "It was more a matter of butter, salt, pepper, corn, and outraged dignity."

Natalie Hays Hammond

At the age of twenty-six, Natalie Hays Hammond participated in an informal debate on the question "Is being born rich a lucky stroke for genius or a bad break?" Sitting opposite her was Albert Spalding, scion of the family behind the sporting goods company. A classical violinist, Spalding argued that he continually had to overcome the impression that he was nothing but a rich dilettante. Natalie Hammond expressed a different attitude. She had no complaints whatever in being the daughter of John Hays Hammond Sr., a mining engineer who had amassed several fortunes exploiting gold in Africa and oil in North America. She liked to make the most of opportunity, even when it was handed to her.

In 1930, Natalie Hammond abandoned high society and a nascent career as an artist to launch the Hammond Process Corporation, basing the company on a method she'd invented for coating fabric with metal.

"It's in the blood," she explained. "I just had to do it. What's a girl to do if she's the innocent victim of heritage? There's no escape for her. So here I am!"

While her older brother, John Jr., actively patented his many inventions, Natalie seemed to prefer abject secrecy for protection. Other inventors have chosen the same route, in the belief that the patent process itself is ultimately a system for publicizing ideas, possibly to the benefit of people who are more creative in the use of that system than in the invention of anything truly new. Natalie Hammond did, however, take out a patent on one of her other inventions, a watch enclosed in a metalwork shell.

The family fortune had helped to open doors for Natalie Hammond—including those of her own factory—but she didn't look at her inheritance as an excuse to loaf. Quite the opposite. "I don't see," she once said, "how a person can justify being alive if he doesn't work."

John Hays Hammond Jr. was also interested in inventions for the kitchen—but then he was interested in inventions of every type. His father, the first John Hays Hammond, had been a mining engineer and one of Cecil Rhodes' associates in the development of vast gold and diamond holdings in South Africa. The Hammonds were rich and preposterously well connected. As the younger Hammond grew up, he met and enjoyed friendships with Thomas Edison, Alexander Graham Bell, Wilbur and Orville Wright, Guglielmo Marconi, and Nikola Tesla—and that was only among the inventors. He mixed with people on the same par in the worlds of literature, government, and music—Rudyard Kipling convinced him to try his hand at fiction.

For a budding inventor, John Jr. had unparalleled opportunities. Remarkably enough, he made the most of them. After graduating from

Yale's Sheffield Scientific School in 1910, Hammond took a low-level job at the U.S. Patent Office. He could have found more glamorous things to do, but he wanted to understand the details of the inventing process and, more than that, to survey the current state of technology. Hammond then moved to his family's summer home in Gloucester, Massachusetts, and launched his fifty-year career in invention. From the start, he was an innovator in radio control, conducting a memorable experiment in 1914 when he sent a boat from Gloucester to Boston and then back. The unusual part of the experiment was that there wasn't a soul onboard. Hammond steered the vessel by remote control from his post in Gloucester.

John Hays Hammond Jr.

Hammond signed over the rights to more than one hundred patents for use by the U.S. government during World War I. With that, he began a long association with the military, supplying technology in such areas as torpedo guidance, propeller control, and ordnance. In his civilian activities, he contributed ideas central to the practical application of broadcast radio. His confidence in invention didn't stop there. He once had some success with a hair tonic for, as he recalled, "a millionaire friend of Pa's, on whose bald head I grew a pink fuzz."

Hammond was an illustrious host, meeting and entertaining new generations of celebrities at the medieval-style castle he built in Gloucester. He was also a gourmet who made himself at home in the kitchen. "Jack Hammond loved to order kitchen gadgets and cook books," recalled Corinne Witham, who was familiar with life at the castle. "When the blender first came out, he asked his secretary to purchase one for the cook to use. When it came, he took the recipe book which came with it, and marked a particular gourmet dessert he wished made for dinner that evening." The cook, who was Finnish, tried her best, but in the end, it was hard to say whether she had more trouble with the strange new appliance or with the English language in which the recipe was written. As Witham wrote in *The Hammond Castle Cookbook*, the cook filled the blender to the brim with all of the ingredients and turned it on, with the result that most of the dessert ended up on the butler, who was standing in the kitchen waiting to serve.

Among the inventions that Hammond created for the kitchen was a bottle opener that enjoyed some popularity, and a pan-free stovetop, which did not. It consisted of layers of foil, and when one was dirty, the cook only had to rip it off and start cooking anew on the sheet underneath. He also invented a syringe for injecting liquids into meat. After a conversation with his friend Clarence Birdseye, who also lived in Gloucester, Hammond came up with a button for frozen food packaging to indicate whether the contents had ever been defrosted.

Hammond remained intrigued with the blender, despite the explosive entrance it made in his kitchen. In the early 1950s, he developed a magnetic mixer, a blender for use in soda fountains. It obviated the very problem that haunted many blenders—leaking at the base of the container where the rotating mechanism connected. Hammond's design called for the container to connect from the top, sticking to an overhang on the blender through magnetic attraction. Hammond received a patent for his blender on September 14, 1954.

In fact, Hammond received two patents that day. One was for the Magnetic Mixer. The other was for a Submarine Attack Computer. For anyone but John Hammond Jr., it would have been remarkable. For him, it was just another day in the lab.

When talking pictures were introduced in 1927–28, theater-goers were left with a problem that even the world's best sound engineers failed to predict: no one could hear what the actors were saying. The voices were coming through the speakers, the Jazz Singer was singing—but it was sometimes downright impossible to hear. The problem lay not in the wiring but in the popcorn. Back when movies were silent, with music to carry the mood, it didn't matter if people in the audience chomped away and, worse, if paper bags crackled. But then talkies came, and when Ruth Chatterton or Ronald Colman was speaking, no one wanted to hear the sound of popcorn bags instead. "Noiseless popcorn bags are the great need of the hour as far as the talking movie public is concerned," wrote a disgruntled fan in Mason City, Iowa, in May 1929. But for a long time, there was no solution. The popcorn stayed the same, and so did the bags.

Popcorn bags were even more annoying when they were empty and in the hands of an impish brat, old or young. In 1946, researchers at the American Paper Goods Company announced the invention of the "pop-proof" popcorn bag. "When the eater blows the bag up as the hero is about to shoot the villain," explained a report on the bags, "he will find the seams will give way before the bag reaches good popping size."

The pop-proof bag didn't catch on. In time, cynics gave up on the problem of noisy popcorn altogether. "A noiseless popcorn bag?" commented the humorist Abe Burrows. "Tell 'em to make it noisier. I can still hear the dialogue." But most movie-goers remained aggravated, until a firm in Sacramento, California, decided to go into the business of frozen orange juice. The plan collapsed, but not before company researchers invented a special package for the product. It consisted of two layers of cellophane insulated with a soft glue. When the company went out of business, 300,000 of the surplus packages were purchased by a San Francisco theater manager named Ira Levin. He planned to use them for popcorn.

Levin had been hunting for a noiseless bag for years. Finally, he had one. The cellophane sheets didn't make a sound as anxious fingers found their way inside to claw up a mouthful of kernels. The bags were seven times more expensive than paper ones, but Levin felt they were worth it. The Hollywood columnist Erskine Johnson made a special trip to San Francisco just to try out the new sensation. "There was no deafening crackle," he confirmed. "I could still hear the dialogue on the screen. The lady sitting next to me didn't stick a hatpin in my ribs and hiss, 'Quiet, you jerk.' She was eating popcorn, too."

Johnson, who suggested that Levin should receive an Academy Award, wasn't entirely kidding when it came to the subject of popcorn bags and movies. "The innovation," noted a business report, "is believed to be drawing buyers who have been reluctant to attract critical glances from neighboring seat holders." Popcorn sales doubled and overall ticket sales increased as patrons enjoyed picture shows in the silence appropriate for a talkie.

After Ephraim Bull introduced the Concord variety in the 1840s, grape growing grew into a national fad. In Vineland, New Jersey, a dentist named Thomas Welch planted a vine in his side yard—although as his son Charles later recalled in a letter written to him, "I remember the grapes you planted on the west side of the house, of the great trellis you thought you needed—a trellis that was climbed more by boys than vines."

Thomas Welch was born in upstate New York and became a physician, though he soon switched to dentistry. He was a staunch church-goer, a Methodist by denomination, but he had a lively sense of adventure withal, moving around the country with his family and sometimes even without them. In 1869, the Welches were settled in Vineland where the dentistry practice was thriving. On Sundays, Welch served as communion steward of his local Methodist Church, a responsibility that presented him with a dilemma. According to the tenets of the church, which he took very seriously, abstinence was a virtue—and yet every Sunday Welch found himself pouring wine for the members of the church. One might think that it was of no import, that the sip doled out in church couldn't make even a flea tipsy. And yet, for some full-grown humans, even a flea-size portion leads to the temptation to have more. A visitor to the Welch home proved the point, apparently going on a bender after starting with just the thimbleful served to him in the church service. Welch was aghast. He told his family that something had to be done and that he was the one to do it.

"That fall," Charles reminded his father in the letter, "in Mother's back kitchen, you experimented with blackberry juice." Blackberries being sweet and heavy, the result probably seemed more like syrup than wine. Experiments turned to Concord grapes, the national favorite: ever available, ever willing. The father and his children squeezed forty pounds' worth and Welch experimented with variations on pasteurization in order to kill the yeast naturally found on the grape skins. It was the yeast that threatened to ferment the juice and taint it with alcohol. The Welches filled twelve bottles with the juice and then waited day after day for the corks to pop off. The corks didn't move, though. The contents were not turning into alcohol or anything else.

Welch slapped labels on the bottles—"Dr. Welch's Unfermented Wine"—and went into business, aiming most of his efforts at churches. His son recalled it for his father: "For two or three years following, you squeezed grapes; you squeezed the family nearly out of the house; you squeezed your family nearly out of money; you squeezed your friends."

The elder Welch stopped squeezing after a few years and went on to other entrepreneurial ventures. His son Charles prudently went into the practice of dentistry, settling in Washington, D.C. But grape juice is, as everyone knows, a hard stain to remove, and within a few years he was back doing the squeezing, restarting a business based on his father's invention. He changed the name from "unfermented wine" to "grape juice" and sold it as a beverage as opposed to a church supply. He thereupon built a business that continues to this day.

Food inventions may be the most common of all. Any original recipe, after all, is an invention. And practically anyone who has spent time in a kitchen has conjured up a new way of making some part of a meal. Hunger is a particularly urgent form of inspiration, especially when punctuated by the realization that the cook forgot to buy a key ingredient.

The fads of the food world keep it from ever settling down. And so, perhaps to an even greater extent than other avenues for invention, the realm of eating will always be ready for something new.

Thomas Welch experimented with variations on pasteurization in order to kill the yeast in grape skins, creating "Dr. Welch's Unfermented Wine," better known as Welch's Grape Juice.

Teressa Bellissimo, seen with her husband, Frank, created Buffalo wings in 1964 in the Italian restaurant the two owned in Buffalo, New York.

Teressa Bellissimo had a problem one day in 1964. No one remembers the exact date anymore, but it was a Friday. And it was in Buffalo, New York. The poultry supplier botched the regular order for the restaurant Bellissimo ran with her husband, Frank and Teressa's Anchor Bar and Italian Restaurant. "We Italians," recalled Frank of that day, "use different types of meat in our sauces, usually I used chicken neckbones. One day my supplier sent me 30 pounds of chicken wings, instead. I laid them out to cut them up, but it wasn't right. I says to myself, 'Isn't that a shame to put those wings in sauce?' So I called my wife, Teressa, and told her I don't think they belong in there."

Food is taken seriously in Buffalo, a city that has been notoriously slow to embrace chain restaurants and other manifestations of the nationalized palate. Homemade, authentic, and/or ethnic food has always drawn the loyalty of Buffalo's diners. Frank and Teressa certainly could not sneak chicken wings into a sauce, not in Buffalo. The wings stayed in the refrigerator.

The Bellissimos' son, Dominic, known as "Rooster," liked to hang around the Anchor Bar with his friends. According to his recollection, he was there late that night, after the Friday night rush was over and the barflies had all gone home. Teressa was in the kitchen. The wings were still in the refrigerator. Rooster came in with news that could not have shocked his mother too much: he and his friends were hungry.

It was in the pause that followed that Teressa apparently decided not to waste any food on them: that is, not any perfectly good, saleable food. She took the wings out of the refrigerator.

No one is certain what happened next in the kitchen at the Anchor Bar, but Teressa Bellissimo came out a few minutes later with the wings, deep-fried and slathered in barbecue sauce, a dish of blue cheese dressing and celery on the side. She had invented Buffalo wings.

In a city that had long kept alive the traditional cooking of cultures from around the world, Teressa Bellissimo gave America a dish to call its own. Rooster and his buddies came back for more whenever they were in the Anchor Bar, other people tasted them, and within a month, according to Frank, the place was selling four thousand pounds' worth of Buffalo wings every week. Thirteen years later, Frank still cried when he told the story.

ELEVATIONS OF TWO DRESSERS, ONE QUITE SIMPLE AND THE OTHER MORE ELABORATE.
SCALE ¾" TO 12".

DETAIL No 2.

THE REQUIREMENTS FOR DRESSERS ARE SO VARIED THAT THE HOUSEKEEPER SHOULD ALWAYS BE CONSULTED WITH REFERENCE TO THE REQUIREMENTS IN EACH CASE FOR KITCHEN UTENSILS, CUTLERY, SILVER, CHINA, TABLE LINEN, FOOD STUFFS, ETC.; ESPECIALLY IS THIS TRUE OF THE LOWER PART, WHERE THE SIZE AND ARRANGEMENT OF COMPARTMENTS AND DRAWERS, AND THE PLACING OF SHELVES CAN SELDOM BE MANAGED SATISFACTORILY WITHOUT CONSULTATION WITH THOSE WHO ARE TO USE THEM. SOME HOUSEKEEPERS WILL REQUIRE KNEADING BOARDS AND A PLACE FOR STORING DINING ROOM EXTENSION TABLE LEAVES IN THE DRESSERS. IN THE FIRST DRESSER SHOWN ABOVE, THE ARRANGEMENT OF FLOUR BINS AND DRAWERS GIVES TOO LITTLE SHELF ROOM IN THE LOWER PART FOR MOST HOUSEKEEPERS, UNLESS THERE WERE PLACE ELSEWHERE FOR KITCHEN UTENSILS.

SCALE (¾" TO 12") FOR SECTIONS A-A AND B-B.

SCALE (3" TO

DETAIL SECTION No 1 FOR GOOD WORK.

DETAIL SECTION No 1 FOR CHEAP WORK.

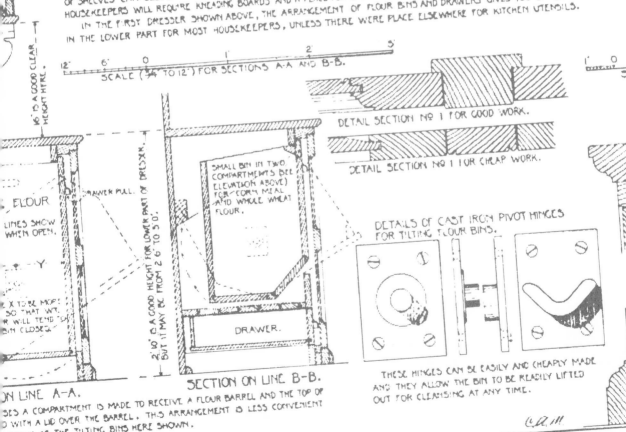

SMALL BIN IN TWO COMPARTMENTS (SEE ELEVATION ABOVE) FOR CORN MEAL AND WHOLE WHEAT FLOUR.

DRAWER.

SECTION ON LINE B-B.

DETAILS OF CAST IRON PIVOT HINGES FOR TILTING FLOUR BINS.

THESE HINGES CAN BE EASILY AND CHEAPLY MADE AND THEY ALLOW THE BIN TO BE READILY LIFTED OUT FOR CLEANSING AT ANY TIME.

ON LINE A-A.

...ES A COMPARTMENT IS MADE TO RECEIVE A FLOUR BARREL AND THE TOP OF ...D WITH A LID OVER THE BARREL. THIS ARRANGEMENT IS LESS CONVENIENT ...LEANLY AS THE TILTING BINS HERE SHOWN.

CHAPTER NINE

Touch and the Physical World

UNLEASHING THE HUMAN BODY

$\mathcal{W}$. C. Soule, a traveling salesman from Savannah, New York, decided one day that people should walk on water. If he felt inspired to go for a turn in the open air, he didn't think it should matter whether he was on land or water. Moreover, as an avid fisherman, he resented the obligation to stand around in shallow water, much preferring the idea of standing on top of it. In 1880, Soule invited members of the press to the Harlem River in what was then a rural part of northern New York City. He promised all comers that he would walk on water.

Soule's invention was the water skate. Dressed in a business suit and a straw boater, the slightly built young man slipped into a pair and his shoes never even drew a splash as he sauntered out onto the river for his

Frank Hill

Frank Hill was ten years old when he went to work in the coal mines of Logan County, West Virginia. The year was 1910. Six years later, the African-American youngster was working next to his friend Charley Miller when he noticed the slate overhead start to crumble. Hill backed away and shouted a warning, but Miller couldn't react quickly enough. He was crushed to death when the slate gave way. Upward of a hundred West Virginia miners were killed in sudden slate falls each year during the first half of the twentieth century, when Frank Hill was in the mines. The increasing use of loud conveyers and mechanical loaders only increased the danger, masking the first crack of the falling slate.

For twenty-four years, Hill thought about the problem of signaling miners just before a slate fall. Whenever he came up with a solution, he described it in a notebook he kept on the subject. When he couldn't come up with any ideas, he just kept thinking. Even after Hill left the mines to become a porter in the West Virginia Statehouse, he continued to work on the problem that he had long since adopted as an obligation. In 1940, he was satisfied that he had the answer: a post attached to the ceiling of the mine with only thin metal strips. When the strips were disturbed, as from movement in the ceiling, a buzzer would sound and bright lights would flash. Hill promised that his Mine Safety and Warning Post would keep any miner from being killed, "unless he wants to."

The state's Mining Safety Commission endorsed the device and the mines chief praised it. With no education, except what he had seen with his own eyes, Hill had solved the problem he set out to conquer.

promenade. The skates were shaped like pontoons, about five feet long, ten inches wide, and five inches deep, and they were hollow, crafted from sheets of zinc soldered along long seams. On the keel of each, Soule's design provided for three sets of flaps (or miniature paddles, as on a water wheel). Hanging by ratcheted hinges, the flaps lay flat when the skate was moving forward, but opened to a perpendicular position whenever it was sliding backward. The action of the flaps allowed Soule to gain traction for each new step. As he strutted around on the surface of the water, his progress was similar to that of a cross-country skier. "The tide was running out at a rate of perhaps two miles an hour," observed one of the reporters in attendance, "but he made his way directly across the stream, and turned and came back to the starting place." Soule admitted that he had no illusions of commercial success for his invention. With the demonstration complete, a rousing success, he returned to his home in Savannah, entitled to boast that he had set out to walk on water, and did.

A dissatisfaction with physical limits is one of the characteristics that describes the human mind. It is also the one that results in the invention of tools, most elementally to extend the powers of the hands and feet. Hands are no doubt useful items, but unencumbered they rank low in the natural world, not as powerful as a bear's paw, as tough as a horse's hoof, or as sticky as a lizard's foot. They await accoutrement: tools serving as a connection between the mind and the world just beyond the touch of the fingers. Inventors, who naturally gravitate toward potential rather than capability in all things, started early providing tools. They show no sign of having tapped every possibility. The feet are somewhat less talented as a rule, but they offer the same satisfaction for the inventor of improving on the human lot with implements that offer not merely a bridge to the outside world but a means of controlling it. That being an instinctual measure of the human experience, the inventor's influence through the millennia has been even more than sociological, it has been anthropological. Survival has not belonged to the fittest, by any means, but to the best equipped. That fact has grown under the general acceleration of the past century, driving a veritable riot of innovation in the field of tools, of which sporting goods may be regarded as a particularly vibrant subcategory.

In dabbling with new sports, Stanley Van Voorhees of California had a nagging frustration with downhill skiing. He didn't like the fact that it required a hill. And he didn't understand why the best part of the fun always had to start at the top; why couldn't a skier have fun at the bottom of a hill? In 1950, Van Voorhees borrowed the technology of the snow track, or its grandfather the tank, to invent self-propelled skis. The skier could go uphill as well as down—"long an appetency of the art," as he wrote very elegantly in his patent application. With Van Voorhees' invention, belts on the bottom of the skis turned, so a skier could go across level land or even traverse a hill. Those belts, however, had to be powered, and to that end, the skier had to carry a small engine in a backpack. The noise, the weight, and the smoke all countered the sport's most appealing sensations, though, making the top of the hill look altogether more attractive again.

Howard Head was not quite so revolutionary, though he did reinvent the equipment in two sports in order to allow people of all abilities to excel.

Before Head, in fact, sporting goods themselves were regarded as part of the challenge; technologically, it was a slow-moving field that catered, if anything, to professionals while letting amateurs follow along and make do. Head, however, had a different idea. "He took a sport that was a certain degree of difficulty and made it less difficult for the players," said a friend.

Raised in an erudite family in Philadelphia, Head was a project engineer at the Glenn L. Martin Co. during World War II, overseeing aircraft manufacturing. In a job summary in 1943, he wrote that his work required "a technical familiarity with all parts and features of an airplane." His training at Martin was the first of three assets that prepared him for a future inventing sporting goods. The other two were more personal: an intense desire to excel at sports combined with a sorry lack of ability. Had Howard Head been a natural athlete, he might not have needed to think so much.

When Head tried skiing for the first time in 1946, he felt clumsy and uncoordinated, even for a novice. After his second ski trip, he pinpointed the problem: the skis, of course. "While on a skiing trip," he wrote soon afterward, "the idea occurred to me of applying to ski design an advanced structural technique developed by the Martin Company during the recent war years." He experimented with a core of aluminum and plywood sandwiched between smooth plastic, eventually replacing the plywood with other natural laminates. After two years of work on the invention, Head entered the market with a ski that was lighter than any of the time-honored wooden ones. Moreover, his ski could hold a much sharper edge. People weren't yet trained to look for the latest in sports equipment. In fact, they typically bought one pair of skis and kept them for life. "I worked for a company that made valves," recalled Inez Foley of a job she had in Cleveland in the late 1940s, "and we would ship them to 'Headski' Company. And I would always say, 'Hey, these are going to that Polish outfit, Headski.'" Head's new firm had to struggle to establish both itself and the radical notion at its core: that the skis made the skier.

Head continually refined the basic invention, perfecting it for the few customers who were willing to pay the steep price of his futuristic skis. "I often thought why Head Ski Company was so successful," reflected a former employee, Chuck Powers, "and why there was so much people-effort. I mean—everybody. Howard had an ability of creating the ski in our minds as the objective. He wasn't the boss; the ski was the boss."

Head skis were expensive, but by the mid-1950s, they caught on, with Howard Head originating new versions in his Baltimore factory.

Howard Head experimented with a core of aluminum and plywood sandwiched between smooth plastic, producing a ski that was lighter than any of the time-honored wooden ones.

In 1964, even traditionalists had to acknowledge that a new era was upon them. Champion racers used Head skis in winning medals at the Olympics in Innsbruck, an indication that the intrepid Howard Head had been right all along.

With some misgiving, Head sold his company in 1970. He settled into a gentlemanly life in a newly acquired, and very sumptuous, Baltimore estate. The property came complete with a tennis court, but unfortunately—or fortunately—Head wasn't as good at tennis as he might have wished. The problem, apparently, was the racket.

At first, Head experimented with small lead weights taped to the edges of the racket in an effort to stabilize the hitting surface. That didn't help very much. "It was the spring of 1974, April actually," Head later recalled, "that the light turned on in my head."

> Literally in the middle of the night, the thought came to me that the idea of adding weights to the rim of the tennis racket to increase stability had been an error. The way to go was to leave the weight alone, but make the racket wider.
>
> I began to zero in on the fact that no matter what I did to improve the racket's stability, I must maintain the integrity of the racket's classic length, weight and balance. These characteristics had grown up over the years and must not be tampered with. Actually, I had learned this in skiing. With skis or any other piece of sporting goods equipment, you must first be careful that you are not making any negative change in the equipment. An experienced user of sporting goods equipment will reject a design that is twice as good in one respect if it's even five percent worse in one that he is used to.

Head took out a piece of paper the next day and drew a sketch of his new invention. While the hitting surface of a standard racket was eight inches wide and ten inches long, he first made the dimensions equal, at ten by ten. That catered to his engineering instincts. Next, his aesthetic sensibility took over and he changed the length, resulting in a surface thirteen inches by ten: the oversized racket. (The United States Tennis Association, the presiding authority in matters pertaining to the sport, did not have any technical specifications for rackets, as it did for tennis balls and courts.)

Head succeeded in expanding the so-called sweet spot of the racket, or as he called it, "the point of percussion," where the reaction of the ball was at its strongest and most predictable. Since hitting a ball was a matter of hand-eye coordination, Head's new racket had the effect of increasing the size of the hand, giving players a more beneficial margin in the attempt to master the game's most basic skill. The unending battle against the body that is at the root of all sports tipped slightly in favor of the frustrated champion within.

Head held a controlling interest in Prince, a company that made practice machines for tennis, and in January 1976 he introduced his new racket under its name. His timing was fortuitous. Tennis was enjoying a boom. Seven million people had starting playing during the previous year alone. Since beginners and anxious intermediates constituted the primary target group for the Prince racquet, it was an instant success. Head's latest invention couldn't make an expert out of a bad player, but it did help a great many people reduce their unforced errors. "I don't think it will ever benefit anyone who has a lousy stroke," observed long-time pro Vic Braden during Prince's first spring. "I contend you can play well with a board if you've got a good stroke. I once saw Bobby Riggs beat a guy with a broom."

Bobby Riggs, the tennis star, was a master of the physical skills of the game. Having started out as a ping-pong champion, he could control a ball, which is to say he could control his own body in the split second of impact. All advanced players could do the same, and yet Riggs, a renowned hustler and show-off, emphasized the point of a physical advantage by winning matches against experienced players using only a broom, frying pan, or umbrella. In addition to being part of Riggs' hustle, his unusual choice of weaponry underscored a fundamentally traditional attitude—to wit, that a good player didn't rely on equipment.

Peavey Tool

"Clumsy cant dogs" gave Maine loggers serious troubles in the 1850s. Logs were transported by river then, sometimes twenty thousand at a time, and they had to be kept in a free-flowing formation. The job of preventing jams fell to the log driver (or river hog), who hopped from log to log, slowing some of them and prodding others, while steering as many as possible in order to keep the whole herd on pace. It was a game, exciting and exhausting. It could also be frustrating, because the barbed poles with which the men guided the logs often let logs get away. The pole was known as the "cant," and the movable hook on the end, which could slip as easily off the log as on, was the "dog." Clumsy cant dogs, though, were just a part of the job in the eyes of the loggers, along with the chance of slipping off a log and falling in the water every once in a while.

In 1858, Joseph Peavey, a blacksmith in the Bangor area, was standing on a bridge over the Stillwater River. Before long, he was lying down on the bridge, watching through the cracks in the boards as the log drivers poked and pushed a large load of logs down-river. Peavey saw what was wrong and knew in a flash how to fix it. He stood up and hurried to his shop, where he directed his son to fashion a new kind of dog, one with a slot for the hook to keep it locked in place against the current. Peavey also insisted that his cant have a spike at the tip. Peavey's invention was finished by the end of the day, and he lost no time in taking it down to the river, where the log-drivers immediately declared it a vast improvement. "In pushing and managing the logs," wrote a visitor at a Maine lumber camp in the 1860s, "the men use pick-poles and 'peaveys,' the last of which are curiously contrived to hold the log as well as send it forward, and it is an invention much admired by the lumberman." John Ross, a veteran logger, announced in public that he could do as much with six men equipped with Peaveys as with twenty men using the old cants. Peavey Manufacturing has survived detrimental trends, such as the advent of railroads and trucks, as well as local disasters, including two factory fires. The company Joseph Peavey founded still makes peaveys, as well as other hand tools, in its Maine factory.

Improvement was directed within, not at the nearest sporting goods store. Prince and Howard Head breached that attitude. Even at the professional level, Head's innovations were eventually adopted as the size and shape of the hitting surface became a frontier for experimentation. If the mediocre could be better, so too could the great.

Howard Head invented skis and rackets but helped to pioneer a new attitude in sport. "He was intrigued literally with everything," said a friend after Head's death in 1991, "from why grass grows to why can't I ski better. He pursued those things because, first he had the interest, then the God-given talent for inventing things or making things different from the way they were being made." From golf clubs to running shoes to pole-vaulting poles, invention became a part of sports in the last half of the twentieth century, in direct response to the simple question as Head posed it: "Why can't I be better?" In the revolution launched by Head skis, every athlete could be just a bit better; innovation pushed the limits of physical ability farther and farther away.

Brother Casimir Zeglen was living in a monastery in Chicago in 1893 when he decided that he could stop bullets. The evidence of millions of deaths through gunfire was wiped away for Zeglen in one flash of horror on October 28 of that year. The same horror was felt by all of Chicago that night as a deranged man called on the city's popular mayor in his home, drew a gun, and shot him to death. While everyone else sought justice through the trial and execution of the assassin, Zeglen imagined how different the outcome might have been if the mayor had been protected, if his skin had been like iron. "I do remember," Zeglen later recalled,

> that it was on the 5th of December, 1893, that I really began work . . . I did not have any definite idea as to just what I was to do to bring about the results which I sought, but I realized, of course, that experiment and experiment only would teach me the facts which I must know before I could hope for success. Undiscouraged, I proceeded with my work, and in the year 1895 by continuous labor and many tests I learned that it was a positive fact that silk dipped in a certain chemical compound known only to myself, possessed in certain degree the property of successfully resisting the shock of a bullet.

Zeglen continued his research even as he maintained his religious duties. To him, his work in the Church and his activities as an inventor were all part of the same devotion to the cause of peace. His dream

Vestproof Bullet

After the bulletproof vest was established as a viable invention early in the twentieth century, death from gunshot ought to have become a statistical anomaly. In actuality, though, use of the vest was concentrated among a fortunate few. While governments concluded that bulletproof vests were too expensive for the average soldier and municipalities lagged in issuing them to policemen, gangsters embraced them with an admirable sense of commitment. As a result, the police found themselves at a disadvantage. They could be shot rather easily, but the gangsters couldn't. No good citizen can abide that state of affairs. But even so, bulletproof vests were expensive; it didn't occur to the good citizens of the 1920s and 1930s to make sure that their police had them.

A Connecticut man named Ernest G. Whipple came to the rescue. In 1935, he invented a vestproof bullet specifically for use by the police. Made of unjacketed zinc, filled with a soft metal, Whipple's bullet promised higher velocity and more rapacious penetration than previous bullets. The vests of the day couldn't stop it. Wolcott Gibbs reported on Whipple's advance for the *New Yorker* magazine, noting that a better vest, impervious even to Whipple's bullets, would inevitably be invented at some point. "And then," Gibbs predicted, "mankind is going to find itself face to face with the horrible dilemma of not being able to kill itself off." As a humanitarian, he was right. With Whipple's achievement, vests and bullets defined one more arena for human confrontation, whether between antagonists in the street or inventors in the lab.

was to produce bulletproof tunics to be worn by soldiers in all of the world's armies, saving lives and foiling battle at its very core. Beyond that, Zeglen had other uses in mind. He was living in times spattered by the specter of assassination and anarchy (as terrorism was known then). "I do not intend this exclusively for military purposes," he wrote of his bulletproof cloth, "but as a protection from the assassin and the madman."

A native of Poland, Zeglen returned home to consult with the expert weavers of his native country. Under their guidance, he devised a means of locking silken fibers together. The new process, combined with the nature of the silk fiber, resulted in Zeglen's announcement in 1897 that he was ready to give a public demonstration of bulletproof cloth. "The secret of the cloth," he said, "lies in the closeness of the weaving." Zeglen could not speak English well and he wasn't prepared for the storm of publicity that met his announcement. Nor was he ready for the man who offered to let marksmen fire on him in the first demonstration, in exchange for a fee of $5,000—which was to be given to his girlfriend if the cloth didn't work.

Zeglen couldn't have that. He stepped in and insisted that he was the one who would stand in as a human target.

Zeglen's superiors, however, couldn't have that. Instead, the first experiment was performed on a cadaver draped in the bulletproof cloth. Thirty rounds from a .44 revolver failed to penetrate the cloth. A .38 weapon, which fires with greater velocity, was found to transmit enough force to break bones, but it did not pierce the cloth. Next, a dog clad in the cloth was shot. The idea of risking the dog's life may be questionable, but the animal survived and trotted away happily once the cloth was unbuckled, apparently regarding the tailored dog suit as more of a nuisance than the gunfire. Finally, it was Zeglen's turn. He stood behind a shield made of the cloth and waited for the fire. No one particularly wanted to fire on the monk in case the cloth failed, but finally an Austrian soldier on a visit to Chicago stepped up with a gun. Zeglen was far less nervous than the soldier or the hundreds of spectators. As the shots rang out, the bullets compressed upon hitting the weave and then bounced harmlessly onto the floor.

Zeglen's bulletproof cloth was extensively tested and found to work against most firearms. Army commanders and law enforcement officers recommended it wholeheartedly, yet it never entered general use on the scale the priest imagined. It was slightly bulky, at about a half inch thick, and moderately expensive. Reluctant procurement officers may not have needed any further excuses to reject it. Reports of Zeglen's successful trials inspired other inventors, though, in the effort to make the body impervious to bullets. Edward C. Gerstenberger of Brooklyn, for example, alternated layers of haircloth saturated with alum and lightweight silesia fabric coated with gutta-percha, a thick gum. He pressed the layers together by means of hydraulic power and produced a fabric that made the human body generally bulletproof— and utterly immobile. Robert F. Stevenson of Silverton, Texas, designed a vest made of aluminum, which had more drawbacks in comparison with the gutta-percha model, being even more constricting and even less bulletproof. Harry Gross of Philadelphia invented a heart shield, consisting of a piece of leather worn in place on a strap around the chest. Even assuming that the leather was strong enough to stop a bullet, Gross' device was best used against attackers with perfect aim. If a bullet missed the heart by any chance, the wearer had every right to be profoundly annoyed.

Brother Zeglen's material was the most practical of its day, but even it was haunted by tragedy and an unfortunate air of irony. In September 1903, President William McKinley was shot at close range by a gunman in Buffalo, New York. McKinley's personal secretary, George Cortelyou, was standing next to the president at the time of the shooting.

"Two weeks before President McKinley was killed," Zeglen noted, "I offered a waistcoat to him, but Secretary Cortelyou stated that the matter could not be considered until the following month."

Another Midwesterner with ties to eastern Europe devoted his life to one of the most basic of tools, the knife. Frank Richtig of Clarkson, Nebraska, was a blacksmith by trade. As an inventor, he was not as concerned with the shape of the knife as with its composition, searching for an alloy of unsurpassed hardness. Nationally known metallurgists were on the same trail using X-ray technology and microphotography to study steel at U.S. Steel's Research Laboratory in Pittsburgh, but Richtig didn't know anything about that. He simply thought he could invent a knife that didn't need to be sharpened so often.

As a teenager, Richtig served a two-year apprenticeship in Nebraska with a blacksmith from Bohemia, where metalworking was art. After opening his own shop in Clarkson, Richtig used his spare time for experimentation, letting the metal teach him what other smiths could not. After twenty years he was finally satisfied, and in the mid-1920s he began making knives by hand in his shop. The handles were made of aluminum, but the blades were steel and so sharp that when the deputies in Cedar Rapids put a padlock on the jail and then lost the keys, they sent for Richtig. He selected a paring knife and sliced through the padlock with a few hits of a hammer. In 1936, a newspaper in Pierce, Nebraska, ran an article about Richtig and his mysterious knives, titling it, "Here's One for Ripley." In time, the famous columnist Robert Ripley answered the call and Richtig had his big break. Ripley drew Richtig in cartoon style and wrote about him in a "Believe It or Not" feature published in papers all over the country.

"Frank Richtig," wrote Ripley in neat block print, "the village smith of Clarkson, Neb. CUTS COLD STEEL—tool steel—auto parts—R.R. spikes—buggy axles, etc. with a BUTCHER KNIFE and then CUTS PAPER with the SAME KNIFE." It was an astonishing claim: a knife so strong that it could be pounded through thick steel without breaking and yet maintain its razor-sharp edge withal.

Each summer, Richtig took to the road to sell his blades. In the midst of the Depression, he sometimes simply stood on a street corner behind a portable table. More often, he rented booths at state fairs,

Blacksmith Frank Richtig in Clarkson, Nebraska, devoted his life to one of the most basic of tools: the knife.

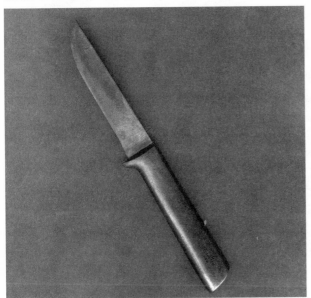

hawking his knives with a simple demonstration that came off, week after week, year after year, just as Ripley had described it. The inventor cut up a great many railroad spikes and sold a great many knives. People could also buy Richtig's wares through the mail as word of the "mystery knives" continued to spread.

For forty years Richtig produced his line of paring knives, butcher knives, cleavers, and bread knives, fashioning each one by hand. A reporter who visited the shop in 1961 watched as he cut the blanks from high-carbon steel and then ground them on emery stones. The next step—the tempering—was the critical one, but Richtig wouldn't say anything about it, nor let the reporter see just exactly what was happening in and around his coal-fired forge. Frank Richtig died in January 1977 without divulging the details of his process to anyone as far as is known. In the years that followed, families in the Midwest passed their Richtig knives on from generation to generation, but otherwise, only knife collectors even recalled the name. In the late 1990s, though, two scientists at the Lawrence Livermore Laboratory in California became intrigued with the claims made for Richtig knives, specifically those recounted in the "Believe It or Not" column. Jeffrey Wadsworth and Donald Lesuer analyzed two Richtig knives in a battery of tests that included tensile stress-strain analysis, chemical composition, determination of hardness, microstructure and isothermal transformation, and surface fracture under strain. With data in hand, Wadsworth and Lesuer concluded that Richtig had developed a two-part tempering process, each stage performed within a very narrow range of temperatures and using various additives to induce subtle changes in the alloy.

The mystery knives only became more mysterious. That process refined by Richtig in his blacksmith shop was apparently the same in most respects as the one introduced by Edgar C. Bain and Edmund S. Davenport at U.S. Steel in a 1930 research paper and a subsequent 1933 patent. While Richtig indicated in a 1969 interview that he had perfected his process in the mid-1920s, the earliest reference to his steel and his knives is the 1936 newspaper article. It is possible that Richtig read the Bain-Davenport patent in 1933 and based his secrets on their conclusions about tempering steel, but it is more likely that Frank Richtig knew some things about metallurgy that might have been news even to U.S. Steel.

In the study at Livermore Labs, Wadsworth and Lesuer couldn't resist having a try at Richtig's famous feat, the one with the railroad spikes and buggy axles—the one that amazed even Robert Ripley. Reducing the challenge just a bit, they tried cutting through a quarter-inch bar of mild steel with a brand-new high-carbon knife. The blade chipped long before the bar gave way. Next, as they wrote, they tried the same experiment again, "hammering the Richtig blade through it." The bar was sliced clean. The Richtig knife survived just as it had on a thousand street corners during Frank Richtig's lifetime: "without damage to the blade."

In 1911, a hungry, frightened man walked out of the wilderness in northern California and broke into a barn. He was cornered inside, right smack in the act of stealing meat. Officials soon realized that the man, estimated to be in his sixties, was no ordinary thief but a Native American who had been living with his tribe in complete isolation in the Sierra Nevada Mountains. With the rest of his tribe having died out, he had been driven out of the mountains by forest fires. And he was practically starving when he broke into the barn. The man, called Ishi after the word for "man" in his native language, knew nothing of Americans and they knew nothing of his stone age civilization.

Far from being prosecuted, he was given refuge at the University of California at Berkeley's Anthropology Department, befriended by three professors there. One of them called him "the most uncontaminated

FIND A RARE ABORIGINE.

Scientists Obtain Valuable Tribal Lore from Southern Yahi Indian.

SAN FRANCISCO, Sept. 6.—Anthropologists of the University of California announce that they have found "the most uncontaminated aborigine in the known world." They have obtained from him, on phonographic records, over 300 words of his language, and expect to exhaust his scanty vocabulary within a week or so. The tribal and folk lore obtained from him thus far is considered of great value.

The man, driven from the mountains by forest fires, was caught near Oroville, a few days ago while attempting to steal meat. "Ishi," as the anthropologists call him, means "man" in the tongue of the Southern Yahi Indians, his tribe. His theory of the origin of fire connects intimately with the mythology of other California tribes and tribes east of the Sierras, and with that of the Greeks and Romans. It involves a superior or supreme being (the coyote) who stole the fire and transmitted it to the Yahis either voluntarily or because he had to do so.

Prof. Waterman offered him a bow and arrow. The old man—Ishi is over 60— brightened up and walked outside. A hat was put on a post 100 feet away, and Ishi sped his first arrow through the centre of its crown. His method of handling the bow is said to be different from that found among any other tribes.

The newspaper article "Find a Rare Aborigine," *New York Times*, Sept. 7, 1911.

aborigine in the known world." By his own choice, Ishi remained at the school, wholeheartedly entering into the task of recording the details of his tribal life. He was as motivated as the professors to save his Yahi Indian culture, if only in the captivity of notebooks and file cabinets. Otherwise, it would die out with him. Sound recordings were made of Ishi's language (which was close enough to another tribal tongue that the academics could communicate with him in a basic way). Offered a bow and arrow, Ishi immediately "brightened up," according to a report. He went outside, where someone put a hat on a post at a distance of about a hundred feet. Ishi held the bow and arrow in a unique manner, but he shot his first arrow straight through the crown of the hat.

Among many other crafts, Ishi described how to make knives from obsidian rock. The trick was to split the rock in one long sweep, so that it created a clean blade, not a serrated one, as was left by the less sophisticated method of tapping off chips in a row.

In surgery, where tools have to be as sensitive as possible in extending the hands, the most modern of instruments today is the obsidian knife, which can be refined to an edge only one molecule wide, making it vastly sharper than a typical stainless-steel instrument or even a Richtig paring knife. Yet it is something of a throwback. As one manufacturer readily admitted in 2007, its obsidian scalpel is "patterned after 'stone-age' knives."

Early obsidian knives have been dated to over one million years ago, surely making them the earliest true invention still in active use. That use was not continual, though, at least not in Western civilization. Two men from different backgrounds and even

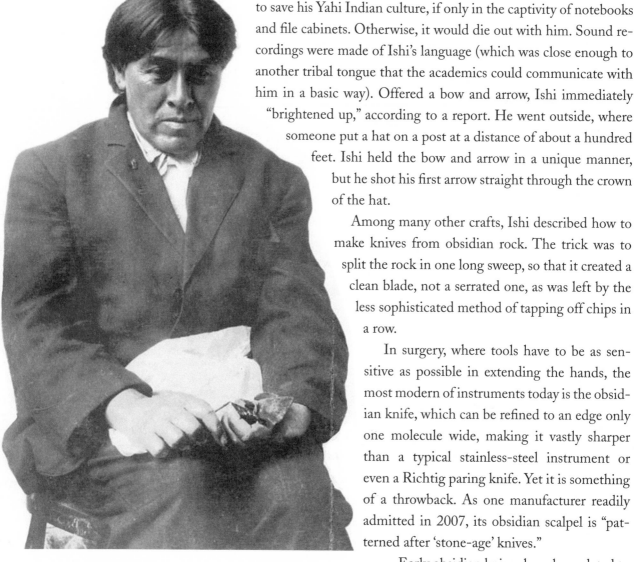

Ishi, a Yahi Indian, described how to make knives from obsidian rock.

from different epochs in human history deserve the credit for bringing the obsidian knife into modern usage. They worked together but never met except in that convergence of ideas by which any two humans might join together, however distant they otherwise are. The first of them was Ishi. He died in 1916 as a result of exposure to tuberculosis, but he left a rich description of his tribe's technique in knife making. The second of the two inadvertent partners was a pickle maker named Donald Crabtree.

In the 1930s, Crabtree started a job as an assistant in the Anthropology Department at Berkeley, working under two of the professors who had recorded Ishi's tribal recollections. Since boyhood, Crabtree had made a hobby of flintknapping—making tools out of rock in the prehistoric manner. He was just the person to receive Ishi's instructions, even as a legacy. Using the aboriginal process invented a thousand millennia before and saved by Ishi, Crabtree became more and more proficient in producing the long, graceful obsidian blade. Continuing to study independently in his native Idaho, Crabtree earned international respect in anthropology circles. That was remarkable since he was by then earning his living as a realtor and pickle manufacturer. Crabtree never stopped trying to replicate ancient methods for producing obsidian knives, however, describing them as the sharpest implements of any material the world has ever known. He admitted that in the process he had cut himself thousands of times and yet, as he said, he didn't mind so much, because the obsidian was so sharp, it didn't bruise adjoining tissue as it cut, making the healing much quicker. In 1968, Crabtree paused in a scholarly article titled "Mesoamerican Polyhyedral Cores and Prismatic Blades" to note:

> One can conclude that men of prehistory had tools which, if used with care, were superior to modern cutlery. Certain surgical needs might be better served if surgeons reverted to using stone scalpels where rapid healing is necessary on types of tissues that are viscid and that resist clean incisions, and where little or no scarring is wanted.

Obsidian scalpel.

Current-day surgical knives made of obsidian.

"The surgeon who pioneers the use of such blades," Crabtree admitted, "may be accused of reverting to cave man tactics, however."

Seven years later, Crabtree faced surgery. Unlike most other patients, he looked at it as a rare opportunity. He used all of the influence at his disposal to convince his surgeons to revert to those very caveman tactics in employing an obsidian blade for the skin incision. Dr. Bruce Buck agreed, using one of Crabtree's obsidian knives to make half of the initial incision; he used a standard steel blade on the other half. Afterward, he termed the experiment a success; the obsidian knife had been easier to use and the incision it made healed at least as neatly. Continuing with further trials on volunteers among his fellow physicians, Buck introduced the idea of using obsidian knives in the hospital setting in a 1982 article in a medical journal. Obsidian blades have since been adopted quite commonly in specialized surgical situations, with studies confirming that they are sharper than standard steel instruments and produce incisions that heal more smoothly in the early stages.

For all of the dedication that surgeons have devoted to improving dexterity, even they couldn't treat it with as much respect as a well-schooled, serious, and slightly desperate card cheat. The best of the sharps rely only on their hands, blindingly quick and sure, but as a group, they are as susceptible as all other human beings to the lure of a shortcut. Gambling inventions are not generally credited to a particular person. In fact, the patent office long refused to grant protection on gambling instruments, on the basis that they "lacked utility." That, of course, was open to debate.

The very best cheating device, after all, is never known to anyone but the inventor. Those that are distributed, however, demonstrate that cheating inspires engineering on a par with any other human endeavor.

In the world of slot machine gambling, Tommy Glenn Carmichael is the world's most famous cheat—or former cheat, fame being an occupational hazard for a man in his profession. In the 1990s, he made his living by inventing implements that induced slot machines to pay out on every spin. He had an array of homemade tools; the ultimate was the "light wand," which he slipped into a machine through the payout slot. It interfered with the light sensor that controlled the payout. After years of taking money out of slot machines at will, Carmichael was arrested in 1998, and as part of his plea bargain, he agreed to keep away from casinos. He subsequently tried to advise slot machine companies on security, but they proved reluctant to let him anywhere near their factories or design rooms.

The world of poker has had its tinkerers, too. "In 1888," recalled a New York editor, "a friend of mine, a professional gambler, told me an illuminating story about a man by the name of Kepplinger." If Leonardo da Vinci understood the human hand as did no other, J. P. Kepplinger of San Francisco was a close second. He had to. As the editor continued, Kepplinger was "an inventor, gambler and cheat."

This friend of mine sat in a game with Kepplinger and three other professionals for several weeks. Of course, the game was supposed to be "straight," because there was no use for a diamond to try and cut diamond and there is supposed to be honor even among gamblers.

But Kepplinger won all the money. The four brother gamblers couldn't understand. They all talked it over together and began watching the German closely. He played in a perfectly natural manner and there was nothing suspicious about any of his movements.

The next day, the other players waited until the game began and then they jumped Kepplinger, tying him to his chair. On searching him, they found an apparatus sewn into the sleeve of his shirt, well concealed by his coat. It gracefully moved forward and took a card out of his hand, or put one there, on cue. The gamblers, having lost fat pots to Kepplinger for weeks, looked down at him with the metalwork, known as a holdout, strapped to his arm. He didn't stand a chance of defending himself. He was entirely at their mercy, as the editor explained.

Instead of thrashing him or killing him, the thoughtful gamblers were enthusiastic over his invention and let Kepplinger off with the promise that he would make each of them one of his "hold-outs."

As a first step in designing the holdout, Kepplinger had ordered a rather peculiar shirt, one with two sleeves on each arm. The sleeves were fitted one over the other and neatly sewn across the top of the cuff to disguise the garment as a standard shirt. The underside, where the two cuffs met, was left unsewn. Kepplinger carefully positioned his holdout between the two sleeves—every fraction of an inch made a difference in the ballet that his hand was to perform. Once he had the holdout where he wanted it, he tacked it in place. He had played plenty of poker in his career and knew what kind of body language drew attention. As a result, he probably could have hidden an elephant on his person without the other players noticing. His holdout relied on that knowledge. When he loosened the tension on a cord on the inner end of the device, a mouth at the other end would open slightly, making for a gap in the unsewn part of the cuffs. At the same time, the clamp that accepted or offered a card (the "thief"), would extend through the mouth and the gap in the cuff, sliding straight into his hand. When it had finished its chores there, Kepplinger pulled on the cord and the thief returned to the inner chamber within the sleeve. Of course, Kepplinger wouldn't want to be seen pulling cords in the middle of a card game. In fact, the line that controlled the holdout ran down under his clothes to his knees. He operated the holdout by spreading his knees or closing them. Kepplinger was so deft in the use of the gadget that the switch was imperceptible.

He had earned thousands of dollars during his streak of artificial good luck, but as an inventor, he had accomplished something even more clever. One can imagine that the holdout might have had other uses through the years, in delicate work of all kinds.

Thousands of Kepplinger holdouts have been sold through gambling catalogs or in casino parking lots over the years. As one catalog boomed, "Kepplinger's Holdout—Most Ingenious Cheating Aid Ever Devised."

To some upstanding citizens, that might have been faint praise. For an inventor, it was an honor worth savoring. Kepplinger had accomplished what he set out to do, and it was as worthy a challenge as any ever set before an inventor. Kepplinger had given the hand nothing less than—another hand. And then there was his craftsmanship. By all accounts, his invention was a beautiful thing to see in operation. Or better yet, not to see.

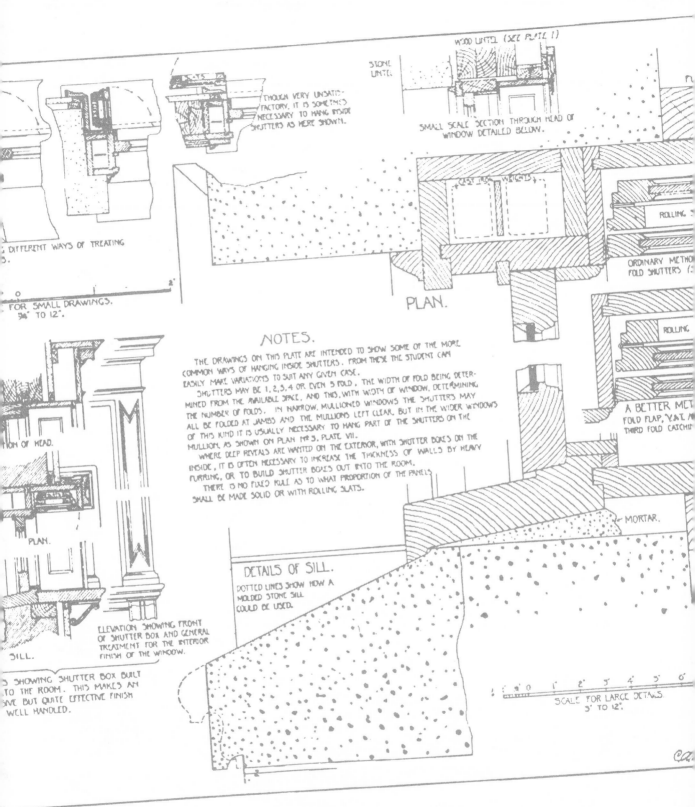

WOOD LINTEL (SEE PLATE I.)

STONE
LINTEL

SMALL SCALE SECTION THROUGH HEAD OF
WINDOW DETAILED BELOW.

CAST IRON WEIGHTS.

PLAN.

ROLLING S

ORDINARY METHO
FOLD SHUTTERS (S

ROLLING

A BETTER MET
FOLD FLAP, Y,&T A
THIRD FOLD CATCHIN

THOUGH VERY UNSATIS-
FACTORY, IT IS SOMETIMES
NECESSARY TO HANG INSIDE
SHUTTERS AS HERE SHOWN.

DIFFERENT WAYS OF TREATING

FOR SMALL DRAWINGS.
¾" TO 12".

0   2'

ION OF HEAD.

PLAN.

ELEVATION SHOWING FRONT
OF SHUTTER BOX AND GENERAL
TREATMENT FOR THE INTERIOR
FINISH OF THE WINDOW.

SILL.

SHOWING SHUTTER BOX BUILT
TO THE ROOM. THIS MAKES AN
VE BUT QUITE EFFECTIVE FINISH
WELL HANDLED.

NOTES.

THE DRAWINGS ON THIS PLATE ARE INTENDED TO SHOW SOME OF THE MORE
COMMON WAYS OF HANGING INSIDE SHUTTERS. FROM THESE THE STUDENT CAN
EASILY MAKE VARIATIONS TO SUIT ANY GIVEN CASE.

SHUTTERS MAY BE 1, 2, 3, 4 OR EVEN 5 FOLD, THE WIDTH OF FOLD BEING DETER-
MINED FROM THE AVAILABLE SPACE, AND THIS, WITH WIDTH OF WINDOW, DETERMINING
THE NUMBER OF FOLDS. IN NARROW, MULLIONED WINDOWS THE SHUTTERS MAY
ALL BE FOLDED AT JAMBS AND THE MULLIONS LEFT CLEAR, BUT IN THE WIDER WINDOWS
OF THIS KIND IT IS USUALLY NECESSARY TO HANG PART OF THE SHUTTERS ON THE
MULLION, AS SHOWN ON PLAN Nº 3. PLATE VII.

WHERE DEEP REVEALS ARE WANTED ON THE EXTERIOR, WITH SHUTTER BOXES ON THE
INSIDE, IT IS OFTEN NECESSARY TO INCREASE THE THICKNESS OF WALLS BY HEAVY
FURRING, OR TO BUILD SHUTTER BOXES OUT INTO THE ROOM.

THERE IS NO FIXED RULE AS TO WHAT PROPORTION OF THE PANELS
SHALL BE MADE SOLID OR WITH ROLLING SLATS.

MORTAR.

DETAILS OF SILL.
DOTTED LINES SHOW HOW A
MOLDED STONE SILL
COULD BE USED.

1'   ½   0   1'   2'   3'   4'   5'   6'
SCALE FOR LARGE DETAILS
3' TO 12".

 CHAPTER TEN

The Larger World

Laws and Long-standing Truths

Ninety-eight cadets entered the Military Academy at West Point with the class of 1876 to be greeted by some of the finest scientific minds in the nation. So stiff were the studies at West Point and so stern the way of life, though, that almost half of the class washed out before graduation. One of West Point's famed teachers was seventy-one-year-old Colonel William H. C. Bartlett, known on campus as "Old Bartlett." Never a man to suffer fools—or freshman—gladly, he was an inspiration to the serious scientists at the school and gave physics students advanced seminars in wave theory long before the concept was even broached at other colleges.

The fifty members of the class of 1876 graduated from West Point in a commencement of earnest speeches and orderly marches. It was otherwise a mild mid-June afternoon along the Hudson. On the very same afternoon, General George Armstrong Custer was on a plain in South Dakota with 277 men, surrounded and then slaughtered by an army of Sioux Indians. West Point's recent graduates were immediately ordered to that desolate plain, the Little Big Horn, to clear the battle-field and replace the fallen troopers.

First Lieutenant Edward S. Farrow was among the newly minted officers rushed to the scene. His first duty was to help bury the dead. His second was to contribute to the investigation of the massacre.

Officers of the Seventh Cavalry pose with wives and a Native American, 1876.

A popular depiction of the Battle of Little Big Horn.

Originally from Maryland, Farrow had intended to serve the military as an engineer, but the army stationed him permanently in the West as a scout, a job that would seem to boast of all the legendary adventure of the frontier. On the contrary, Farrow was generally tied to army posts, and he found that life at the posts bored everyone to the point of distraction. Farrow had a lively mind and he took an interest in Indian culture and in trekking, but overall, he couldn't find enough to do, a fact borne out by the title of a volume he wrote while he was stationed out West: *Pack Mules and Packing*.

While Farrow was packing and unpacking mules at the Vancouver Barracks in Washington State in 1881, others passed the time by experimenting with spiritualism. Farrow had no use for a belief in the netherworld, but nonetheless, he found that he had to participate in nightly sessions with Ouija-type boards and levitation. There wasn't anything else to do.

Night after night, captives to the isolation of the Vancouver Barracks collected in the roughly furnished officers' quarters to delve into their experiments. One that was regularly a success had four people touching their fingertips to a small board, or "planchette," in the center of the table. With nothing lifting it from underneath, the board rose into the air. That wasn't the phenomenon that haunted Farrow for the rest of his life, though. He recalled that three men sat on top of the table, while a woman stood on the fourth side and placed her fingertips on the edge. By some means, the table then rose into the air, with the men atop. Farrow couldn't explain what had happened, even though he'd been there.

Edward Farrow possessed an inventor's mind. Before his career was through, he would originate a convertible camp bed and over twenty components for various types of pistols. But those were mere improvements. He harbored an even grander ambition, one planted during the long nights at the Vancouver Barracks. The possibility that fascinated him more than any was that of breaking through the confines of the physical world—although not with the help of any ectoplasm. He wanted to find a scientific way to defy gravity.

Invention has the power to redraw the common understanding of nature. Cunning inventors build on the laws of physics, which are immutable, but at the same time, they fashion objects and processes that find a way to them anew, on the tenet that the only limits reside in the mind.

A European priest arrived in America early in the twentieth century with just such a startling invention, one that was launched from his own unique attitude toward the universe. Father Manuel António Gomes grew up on an impoverished farm in Portugal. His passion for science was one factor in his decision to become a priest, the seminary offering an education that he couldn't hope to receive elsewhere. After he was ordained, his superiors assigned him to teach college and allowed him time for research as well. Because he was a tall person, his friends nicknamed him "Himalaya." He liked the name so much, he used it the rest of his life.

Father Himalaya had sophisticated knowledge in a wide range of subjects, from botany to astronomy to wave dynamics, demonstrating that his studies had taken him a long way from the farm. And yet the economy of his boyhood world remained with him. A farm is itself a type of machine, and when it is operated efficiently, everything has value; nothing need be wasted. Father Himalaya brought the same sense to his study of the universe. Though the prevailing wisdom was that the only energy sources for the earth came from the earth (mainly in the form of wood, coal, and oil), Father Himalaya stretched that view. He believed that the earth was closely connected to the universe and that astronomy was more than a study of distant lights. Moreover, in his own experience, he was distressed by the use of wood as a primary source of fuel for energy, having seen the decimation of forests in his native country. Other inventors had attempted to exploit the fact that the sun radiated a usable

Father Manuel António Gomes' pyrheliophor was big news at the Louisiana Purchase Exposition, 1904.

form of energy, building solar collectors that could absorb energy as heat to be stored in water or some other liquid and then used to run machines. The early efforts were generally underpowered, though; they couldn't generate the high temperatures needed for viable operation.

In 1904, Father Himalaya arrived in the United States with plans to build his new invention, a solar collector capable of producing higher temperatures than any manmade device ever had. The prime venue for unveiling a revolutionary invention was a world's fair, and America happened to be hosting one that year. It was the Louisiana Purchase Exposition, otherwise known as the 1904 St. Louis World's Fair. Father Himalaya's native country, Portugal, wasn't prosperous at the time and didn't even have an exhibit at the fair, but Father Himalaya was accorded exhibit space nonetheless. All he had to do was transport his invention, which was the size of a barn. Fortunately, a sponsor stepped up with $4,000: a brilliant physics student named Emilia dos Santos, who also happened to be rich.

Souvenir book from the Louisiana Purchase Exposition, 1904.

Father Himalaya, then thirty-six, had built three collectors before, but never on the scale he envisioned for St. Louis. He spent the summer reconstructing it on the fairgrounds: a structure of iron beams and struts, standing forty-three feet tall at the highest point. Looking like a slightly drunken version of the Eiffel Tower holding up a glassy reclining chair, the apparatus baffled fairgoers who happened on it during construction. Father Himalaya laughed when someone asked if it was a machine for drying clothes. Someone else thought it was an airship. One inexplicable guess suggested that it was a dunking chair, one for outsized witches, apparently.

The inside of the concave "chair" was covered with 6,117 mirrors, set in a pattern that Father Himalaya had designed "with mathematical principles," according to one description. The entire structure turned to follow the sun while the mirrors redirected its beams toward a heating surface about six inches in diameter. A crucible in the form of a barrel was situated beneath. In October, after five months of construction—and a great many broken mirrors—the structure was finished and Father Himalaya was ready for the first trial. He was a relaxed person by nature, but even so, he must have been aware that he was undertaking a high-wire act: one slip and he would fall into the abyss of international ridicule. His own reputation was the least of his problems. His country's honor was at stake. And so was Madame dos Santos' money. With great fanfare—world's fairs allowing for nothing less—he announced that he would demonstrate his invention for the first time ever on October 18.

Reporters from all over the country duly arrived, along with fair officials and spectators, to see the machine in action. "For the benefit of those who wish to forget the name of this instrument," commented a newspaper writer, "it has been christened the pyrheliophor."

In ancient Greek, *pyrheliophor* means "fire sun I bring." Unfortunately, the day of the grand debut in St. Louis was cloudy and then foggy, which is not good weather for fire sun bringing. Father Himalaya, however, was unperturbable, and the pyrheliophor turned out to be the same. It took a wide bite of sunlight and focused it into the crucible, creating a temperature within that was measured at 6,800 degrees Fahrenheit, a world record for induced heat and more than enough to turn iron into a molten liquid. "I feel compensated," Father Himalaya said afterward.

Demonstrations of the pyrheliophor—the "sun machine," as they called it in Missouri—continued daily, and at the exposition's conclusion, the International Committee awarded its highest prize to the pyrheliophor. Father Himalaya remained in the United States to pursue his scientific interests, confidently announcing that the pyrheliophor proved that the sun's rays are electrical (which is not actually true). He was right in another of his conclusions, though, regarding the pyrheliophor's potential for powering steam engines in regions flooded with sunlight. "Here would seem to lie the solution of the fuel problem," commented an editorialist in 1904. To that end, Father Himalaya was besieged with offers from people hoping to capitalize on the pyrheliophor, but he shied away from them. He wasn't a money man, just an inventor, and he knew it. "I feel sure," he responded, "in such a great country as America, with its immense wealth and immensely interesting people, there will be some one to find this work of value without deceiving themselves or allowing others to deceive them and fill them with regret. Even if I never reach with the sun machine the end to which I am working, some one by aiding the research will be a benefactor of humanity." Commercialism may not have held any interest for Father Himalaya, but without a profit motive, no one stepped forward to support further research. Father Himalaya eventually returned to Portugal and was then assigned to Brazil, where he concentrated on botanical experiments.

The pyrheliophor was a behemoth in every way, worthy of its role as the host of the sun on the surface of the earth. For a year or two, Father Himalaya's invention had captured the imagination of the public, long convinced that energy from the sun was too weak to be of use by the time it entered the earth's atmosphere. Making a good picture in the papers and an even better caption, with its silent ability to melt iron or granite, the sun machine proved that solar energy, controlled by precise thinking, was anything but weak.

When Edward Farrow retired from the army, he was still haunted by his fascination with gravity and finding a means to counteract it. Farrow believed that science could offer an explanation, and if it did, he would be able to replicate the phenomenon of levitation he'd seen—or thought he'd seen—at the Vancouver Barracks. Returning east after twenty years in the Wild (and very dull) West, Farrow became in inventor and military consultant in New York. The man who had started his career at Little Big Horn, plucking arrows out of dead soldiers, helped to develop gas and aerial warfare tactics during World War I. A few years earlier, in 1911, he had dedicated time to his earlier fascination with levitation. Harking back to his studies with Old Bartlett at West Point, he decided to use electrically generated waves—more specifically, the long, versatile waves discovered by Heinrich Hertz in 1887. Farrow worked with another West Point disciple of Bartlett's, General George Eaton, who had been a cavalry officer during the Indian wars in the Southwest. The two veterans of the West consulted on the problem for several years. In 1911, Farrow completed a working invention, which he described as "a mechanical means to suppress gravity."

In November 1911, Farrow was ready to give a demonstration of the invention. With his laboratory filled with New York reporters and scientists, he suspended a book from a scale and noted that it weighed 15 ounces. He then attached a box called the "condensing dynamo" to the book, apparently without affecting the weight of the book. As he turned a switch, the wheels inside the dynamo began to turn. Farrow explained his theory: that the dynamo was intensifying, or condensing, Hertzian waves and dispersing them horizontally. They then interfered with the vertical force of gravity, according to Farrow. In any case, observers watched as the indicated weight of the book dropped by three ounces, or one-fifth. "This is revolutionary—even sensational," marveled one of the editors invited to see the invention in action. It almost certainly wasn't antigravity, though, not in the sense Farrow intended. Still, he had found some way to mitigate the forces of gravity, which had been his goal from the start, back at Fort Vancouver.

Farrow's condensing dynamo wasn't patented and no plans for it have ever surfaced, but modern speculation has accepted that it was based around electromagnetics. If so, Farrow was already lagging behind a certain college sophomore in Worcester, Massachusetts. There was no shame in that—everyone lagged behind Robert Goddard. An exceptional student, especially in the sciences, Goddard was already fascinated by long-range rockets, a field he would advance with his greatest inventions as an adult. In 1906, as a twenty-four-year-old, Goddard responded to a college assignment to write a fictional story about transportation nearly fifty years in the future. Goddard imagined a high-speed railroad lifted in the air by electromagnets and pulled through a tube. The drawback was that passengers might feel as though they were riding in a pneumatic tube, like the ones that deliver deposit slips at a bank's drive-in window. They might not mind, though: young Goddard promised that passengers leaving New York would arrive in Boston ten minutes later.

In the short story, Goddard's hero, Maurice Sibley ("pre-eminently a genius," yet "highly entertaining"), explained the potential of the train as it prepared for its maiden run:

> Just a word or two regarding propulsion, and we are off. From those metal boxes, of which you see three at each end of the car, there project strong electro-magnets, actuated by a number of specially constructed storage battery cells beneath the floor. The car is propelled, in brief, by the repulsion between these magnets and three rows of similar magnets placed in the sides and roof of the tube from one end to the other. . . .
>
> It does not require much investigation to see the wonderful capabilities of speed which this mode of travel offers. As the magnets at the sides of the car are strongly repelled by those projecting from the tube immediately below them, the whole car is lifted, so that there is no material in contact with it,—in fact it would require considerable force to press the car down in contact with this row of magnets.

Sibley—or Goddard—had even solved the problem of energy for the magnets. "Although they require considerable power," Goddard wrote, "this is furnished cheaply by a battery of wave motors off the Long Island coast."

Goddard liked the idea so much, he submitted it to *Scientific American*, probably his favorite magazine and one he'd been reading since receiving a gift subscription as a young boy. In 1909, it published a shortened version of Goddard's plan, "The Limit of Rapid Transit."

Goddard didn't exactly invent the levitated train, any more than Jules Verne invented the nuclear submarine (though Goddard was motivated, late in life, to revisit his youthful idea and apply for a patent on

Robert Goddard, an American physicist and a pioneer in modern rocket research, with one of his inventions.

it). More important, as a student, he typified the millions of people who had imagined just how smooth and fast a train could be if only it were relieved of the drag of wheels on the rail—if only it could float on air. James Powell was one of the millions.

In a traffic jam one summer night in 1960, Powell had the inspiration, and certainly the time, to dream about an airborne train. He also had the expertise, being employed at the Brookhaven National Laboratory on Long Island as a physicist with a specialty in high-powered magnets. Powell discussed his initial ideas with a colleague, Gordon Danby, and the two developed a practical system for lifting a train into the air, just a little. It called for the installation of superconducting magnets along the bottom of the train, which would envelop a U-shaped guide along the center of the track. The magnets would repel the guide, just to the extent of lifting the train about three-eighths of an inch off the ground. Their system was called magnetic levitation, shortened to "maglev," a name that seemed to lend the system Russian ancestry.

In 1966, Powell and Danby publicly introduced the invention, making the bold assertion that "the concept is technically and economically feasible with present materials." Detailed calculations supported their confidence in the maglev, and the Department of Transportation cautiously began to investigate the possibilities, granting contracts for further study. Stanford University undertook one of the government-sponsored studies. During protests against the Vietnam War in 1970, an office at the school sported a sign that read, "Maglev, Not War." Those who knew what it meant thought it was terribly clever.

Powell and Danby still considered themselves to be on the research side of the maglev question themselves. In 1971, they presented an addition that completed the elegance of their solution to the need for high-speed transit. Powell and Danby designed a separate system of synchronized magnets to propel the train to speeds as high as 300 mph. Henry Kolm, a physicist at MIT, explained that a train driven forward by the system would be akin to a "magnetic surfboard riding the forward slope of a traveling magnetic wave."

Henry Kolm, a physicist at MIT, explained that a train driven forward by the magler system would be akin to a "magnetic surfboard riding the forward slope of a traveling magnetic wave."

A project the size of an intercity maglev required government sponsorship. Over the course of more than thirty years, the U.S. government alternately studied the possibility and canceled all funding for such studies. Meanwhile, Japan, Germany, and China each constructed maglevs and are operating them successfully. The trains are, as Powell and Danby promised, quiet, fuel-efficient, and easy to integrate into an urban landscape. Daniel Patrick Moynihan, the late senator from New York, couldn't understand the indifference. He wrote an article for *Scientific American* called "How to Lose: The Story of the Maglev." The theme, as he wrote, was that "the United States had invented a wholly new mode of transportation but was watching others put it to

Gordon Danby and James Powell developed a practical system for lifting a train into the air called "magnetic levitation," shortened to "maglev." Courtesy of Brookhaven National Laboratory.

THE SPIRIT OF INVENTION

A maglev train.

use." Powell and Danby invented other technology, separately or together. Danby was largely responsible for transforming the magnetic resonance imaging (MRI) machine into an open loop rather than a claustrophobic tunnel. Powell invented the particle bed reactor for use in nuclear fission facilities. Yet they were as frustrated as the most neophyte inventor trying to interest someone, anyone, in their native country in a truly invaluable idea. "Magnetic levitation is the most important development in transportation since the airplane," insisted Moynihan. The two inventors remained undaunted over the years, willingly speaking to any group of officials who might support the maglev in America. "One thing that frustrates Jim and me," said Gordon Danby, "is that we go and give talks on our whole concept, and it's invariably well received, and yet the people who judge these things have already made up their minds."

For almost a century, light energy was understood to be chaotic, a continuing explosion of electrons spreading merrily to illuminate all but the farthest corners and the most well-shielded shadows. The invention of the laser in 1960, however, proved quite the opposite to be possible.

Laser light bears itself in a single direction, as opposed to the splayed disposition of all other light. The concept was proposed in principle in a 1958 article by Charles Townes and Arthur Schawlow, two scientists associated with Bell Laboratories. Townes also taught physics at Columbia University. The article, published in the *Physical Review*, built on theories originating with Albert Einstein as well as practical success in training microwaves. It suggested that some kind of crystal could be used in conjunction with a pair of mirrors situated at either end to produce light amplification by stimulated emission of radiation—*laser* in the acronym. "We thought it might have some communications and scientific uses," Schawlow said later, "but we had no application in mind. If we had, it might have hampered us and not worked out as well."

Charles Townes.

No one else was quite sure what the laser could do either, yet practically every big research lab wanted to be the first to have one, to turn the outline offered by Townes and Schawlow into a reality. In addition to Bell Labs, the Massachusetts Institute of Technology, Columbia University, General Electric, RCA, and IBM all poured resources into the effort to produce the first workable laser.

The Hughes Aircraft Company joined the fray in its own wan attempt, earmarking a relatively paltry $50,000 for research at its lab in Culver City, California. Theodore Maiman, a thirty-three-year-old senior physicist, was assigned to work on the problem. In 1960, he decided to experiment with synthetic ruby as the crystal component, even though data accepted in the field indicated that it was among the least efficient of all substances in stimulating the molecular activity inherent to the laser. "But I had a hunch that other people were not investigating the ruby thoroughly," Maiman later recalled. He made calculations that encouraged him to concentrate on the synthetic ruby. He also implemented a pulsing energy source to reduce the heat buildup. Even as it was, heat in the crystal was so basic a problem that the experiment had to be performed at minus 196 degrees Centigrade (minus 321 degrees Fahrenheit).

Arthur Schawlow.

The laser in theoretical terms had a long line of inventors. As of 1960, it had one in practicality. Maiman became the first person to produce a laser beam, if only for a span of 1/2,000th of a second at a time. Nonetheless, it was light and it was well behaved, a red beam that did not stray from its mark. Maiman's invention was soon followed by others, emitting a steadier beam, using crystal or gas as the emitter.

Press reports explained that a laser was so tightly focused that from the earth it could illuminate a tract of land on the moon only a yard square. Moreover, it could burn a hole in flesh or permanently blind a person. After World War II and the epoch-making invention of the atomic bomb, people immediately thought of it as a weapon, and the press took to calling the laser the "death ray." At a party in Los Angeles, Maiman was introduced to Bette Davis. "How does it feel to have invented something," asked the actress, "capable of bringing such destruction to mankind?" He said he didn't know exactly. Later, when a reporter asked Maiman if the laser could actually become a death ray, the inventor replied again that he didn't know.

In the early 1960s, no one was absolutely sure how to utilize the new tool. "A laser," as Maiman said in 1964, "is a solution seeking a problem." Within decades, it would become the beacon of its age, carrying data to speed communications and offering a gentle kind of burnisher or knife in medicine. At the start, the uses weren't as important a motivation as the raw desire to control all that could be controlled within the bounds of the laws of physics. Convincing light to behave was tantamount to turning the ocean into a gentle river. If it seemed impossible, it was all the more irresistible as a quicker route into the future.

Any inventor who can change the perception of the possible in relation to the physical world can stand perfectly still afterward and let a new epoch come to the invention.

Notes on Sources

CHAPTER ONE

Automatic Indicator: "The Latest Wonder—the Telephone Outdone," *Cincinnati Commercial*, Apr. 10, 1880, p. 3. **General Daniel Ruggles:** "A New Method of Precipitating Rain Falls," *Scientific American* (Feb. 1, 1881), p. 5. **Miss Skerritt:** "Steps for Coaches," *Indiana (PA) Progress*, June 23, 1881, p. 22. **Henry Staats:** "An Invention Destined to Supersede Rowing," *Fort Wayne Gazette*, Aug. 27, 1881, p. 2. **John McAdams:** "A Curious Device," *New York Herald*, Sept. 17, 1882, p 1. **Albert Fearnaught:** "A Singular Invention," *Newark (OH) Daily Advocate*, Oct. 2, 1882, p. 3. **Sauerkraut nosepad:** "Cabbage," *Burlington (IA) Weekly Hawk Eye*, Apr. 29, 1980, p. 11; untitled article, *Athens (OH) Messenger*, Dec. 23, 1880, p. 6. **Eli Whitney:** "Correspondence of Eli Whitney Relative to the Invention of the Cotton Gin," *American Historical Review* 3, no. 1 (Oct. 1897), p. 93. **Robert Fulton:** "Why Robert Fulton Is Acclaimed as the Inventor of the Steamboat," *New York Times Magazine*, Sept. 26, 1909, p. 2. **Band saw:** Rodney C. Loehr, "Saving the Kerf: The Introduction of the Band Saw Mill," *Agricultural History* 23, no. 3 (July 1949), p. 170. **Minister quoted on invention:** "Sermon by Rev. C.S. Nickerson," *Waukesha (WI) Journal*, Mar. 29, 1890, p. 8. **Perpetual motion sidebar:** "Baffled by Perpetual Motion," *New York Times*, Feb. 7, 1894, p. 2; "Man in Motion," *Newsweek*, 82 no. 19 (Nov. 5, 1973), p. 84.

CHAPTER TWO

Gertrude Forbes: Mike Bird, "Lady Inventor," *Pasadena Independent Star-News*, Mar. 2, 1958, p. 47. **Harold Edgerton:** Associated Press, "Inventor of Modern Strobe Photography, 84, Still at It," *Frederick (MD) Post*, Dec. 28, 1987, p. 25; Andy Grundberg, "H.E. Edgerton, 86, Dies; Invented Electronic Flash," *New York Times*, Jan. 5, 1990, p. B4. **Cromwell Dixon:** "Cromwell Dixon, Daring Young Man on Motor Kite, Flew Across Divide 46 Years Ago," *Helena Independent Record*, Sept. 29, 1957, p. 7; "Boy Prodigy of the Air," *Washington Post*, Oct. 8, 1907, p. 6; C. M. Deardurff, "A Sky Bicycle," *Technical World*, Mar. 1908; "Story of Cromwell Dixon Recalled by Arrival of His Sister in Capital City," *Helena Independent Record*, July 26, 1964, p. 19; Hargis Earlywine, "New Discoveries About the Oldest Toys," *Lima (OH) News*, Dec. 25, 1960, p. 12; "Killed in West,"

Lima (OH) News, Oct. 3, 1911, p. 1. **A. C. Gilbert:** John Bainbridge, "American Boy," *New Yorker*, Dec. 20, 1952, p. 36; Roy Nuhn, "Make Lots of Toys," *American History Illustrated* 50, no. 8 (Dec. 1980), p. 39; Max K. Gilstrap, "Toys that Teach," *Christian Science Monitor*, Jan. 31, 1942, p. 4; "Just a Boy," *Time* 77, no. 6 (Feb. 3, 1961), p. 76. **John Lloyd Wright:** Erin K. Cho, "Lincoln Logs: Toying With the Frontier Myth," *History Today* 43 (April 1993), p. 31. **Lego:** Tom Atwood, "Lego Mindstorms," *Robot* (Fall 2005). **Idaleen Root:** "World Beats Path to Door of Inventors," *Sheboygan (WI) Press*, Nov. 20, 1936, p. 21. **Albert Gelardin:** Hal Booyle, "Gadgeteer Finds There Is Money in Small Devices," *Fresno Bee*, Dec. 22, 1954, p. 7. **John Jay Osborn:** "Vacuum Cleaner and Garters Go Into $15 Electric Organ," *Sheboygan (WI) Press*, May 23, 1936, p. 19. **Frank Epperson:** "Spelling," *Oakland Tribune*, Feb. 8, 1959, p. 101. **Joseph Francis:** "Inventor of the Lifeboat," *New York Tribune*, reprinted in *Galveston News*, Aug. 20, 1886, p. 13; "Tribute to Dr. Francis," *New York Times*, Apr. 2, 1891, p. 3; "Youth's Department," *Wellsboro (PA) Agitator*, Oct. 7, 1896, p. 4. **Ernest Patrick:** "Kentucky Mountain Boy Inventor Claims First Tubeless Radio Today," *Coshocton (OH) Tribune*, Apr. 7, 1932, p. 16. **Philo Farnsworth:** "Boy Inventor Has Diskless 'Televisor,'" *Decatur Daily Review*, Sept. 31, 1928, p. 4; Donald G. Godfrey, *Philo T. Farnsworth: The Father of Television* (Salt Lake City: University of Utah Press, 2001); "Farm to Fame," *BusinessWeek*, Dec. 11, 1943, p. 36; David E. Fisher and Marshall Jon Fisher, *Tube: The Invention of Television* (Washington, D.C.: Counterpoint, 1996); Albert Abramson, *Zworykin, Pioneer of Television* (Urbana: University of Illinois Press, 1995).

CHAPTER THREE

Scientific American: "Introduction to Volume II," *Scientific American* 2, no. 1 (Sept. 26, 1846), p. 1; "Information Wanted," *Scientific American* 2, no. 1 (Sept. 26, 1846), p. 5; "Hard Climbing," *Scientific American* 2, no. 1 (Oct. 10, 1846), p. 1; "Progress of Inventions Since 1845," *Homeston (IA) New Era*, Oct. 16, 1889, p. 8; "General Chat By Lightning," *Scientific American* 2, no. 1 (Sept. 26, 1846), p. 2; David A. Hounshell, "Public Relations or Public Understanding?: The American Industries Series in *Scientific American*," *Technology and Culture* 21, no. 4 (Oct. 1980), p. 589; *Popular Mechanics*: Jules Verne, "Future of the Submarine," *Popular Mechanics* 6 (June 1904); Winston Churchill, "Fifty Years Hence," *Popular Mechanics* (Mar. 1932); W. B. Kaempffert, "Miracles You'll See in the Next Fifty Years," *Popular Mechanics* 93 (February 1950); Mary Seelhorst, ed., *The Best of Popular Mechanics, 1902–2002* (New York: Hearst Communications, 2002). **Crystal Palace:** "The Crystal Palace," *New York Times*, July 16, 1853, p. 4; "The Great Exhibition," *New York Times*, July 22, 1853, p. 1; Robert C. Post, "Reflections of American Science and Technology at the New York Crystal Palace Exhibition," *Journal of American Studies* 17 (1983), p. 337. **1876 Centennial Exhibition:** "The Machinery Hall," *New York Times*, Feb. 6, 1876, p. 1; Dee Brown, *The Year of the Century: 1876* (New York: Scribner, 1966). **Purdue University:** Horton Budd Knoll, *The Story of Purdue Engineering* (West Lafayette, IN: Purdue University Studies, 1963); H. W. Wiley, "The Earliest Dynamo," *Science* 67, no. 1743 (May 25, 1928) pp. 532–3. **University research institutes:** A. A. Potter, "Research and Invention in Engineering Colleges," *Science* 91, no. 2349 (Jan. 5, 1940); "Invention Grants Under Attack," Associated Press, Mar. 14, 1975, p. 4; Jeannette Colyvas, et al., "How Do University Inventions Get into Practice?" *Management Science* 48, no. 1 (Jan. 2002), p. 61. **Inventors' contest sidebar:** "An Adolescent Edison?" *Outlook and Independent*, Aug. 19,

1929, p. 613; "1929 Edison Test for Boys Revealed," *New York Times*, Feb. 12, 1940, p. 16; Patricia Sullivan, "His Youth Brightened by Edison, Physicist Reached for Mars," *Washington Post*, June 4, 2006, p. C7.

CHAPTER FOUR

Menlo Park: "Some of His Neighbors Don't Believe That He is Such a Wonder, After All," *New Philadelphia (OH) Democrat*, Dec. 13, 1894, p. 7; "Edison at Home," *Telegraph Journal*, April 15, 1878, 166; Matthew Josephson, *Edison: A Biography* (New York: McGraw-Hill, 1959); "An Inventor's Workshop," *New York Times*, Aug. 9, 1880, p. 8; William Joseph Hammer, "Edison—Man and Genius," *Philadelphia Record*, October 20, 1931, p. 12D; William J. Hammer typescript memoir, collection 69, series 1, box 16, folder 3, Archives Center, National Museum of American History, Smithsonian. **Aiken family:** Richard M. Candee, "Illustrating Invention: Nineteenth-century Machine Advertising for the Aikens of Franklin, New Hampshire," *Printing History* 20, no. 1, p. 12. **General Electric:** W. R. Whitney, "Research as a Financial Asset," *General Electric Company Review* 14 (1911), p. 328; R. L. Duffus, "A Workshop of Science," *New York Times*, July 6, 1930, p. 106; Will Lissner, "Research by GE at Vast Cost Told," *New York Times*, Mar. 13, 1946, p. 30; "Edison Astonished as Science Wizards Show New Marvels," *New York Times*, Oct. 19, 1922, p. 1. **William Coolidge:** Jill Gerston, "William D. C. Coolidge, 101, Dies," *New York Times*, Feb. 5, 1975, p. 40. **Katharine Burr Blodgett:** Edna Yost, *American Women of Science* (Philadelphia, PA: Lippincott, 1955). **Charles Steinmetz sidebar:** Charles Steinmetz, "Electricity and Civilization," *Harper's Monthly* 144 (Jan. 1922), p. 227; "Story of Steinmetz," *New York Times Magazine*, Nov. 1, 1908, p. 9; International News Service, "Lightning Created in Laboratory of Electric Company," *Newcastle News*, June 6, 1923, p. 10. **Mary Ann Strehlein sidebar:** Carol Kleiman, "Working Woman," *Chicago Tribune*, Jan. 10, 1968; Stacy V. Jones, "New Garment Fastener," *New York Times*, Dec. 23, 1967, p. F33.

CHAPTER FIVE

Karl Jansky: Harald T. Friis, "Karl Jansky: His Career at Bell Telephone Laboratories," *Science* 149 (Aug. 1965), p. 841. **Grote Reber:** Grote Reber, "A Play Entitled *The Beginning of Radio Astronomy*," *Journal of the Royal Astronomical Society of Canada* 82, no. 3 (Jun. 1988), p. 93. **Naval Consulting Board:** Lloyd N. Scott, *Naval Consulting Board of the United States* (Washington, D.C.: Government Printing Office, 1920). **Naval Research Laboratory:** Ivan Amato, *Pushing the Horizon: Seventy-Five Years of High Stakes Science and Technology at the Naval Research Laboratory* (Washington, D.C.: Naval Research Laboratory, 1998); Naval Research Laboratory, *Highlights of NRL's First 75 Years, 1923–1998* (Washington, D.C.: Naval Research Laboratory, 1998); "New Navy Invention Tells Ocean Depths," *New York Times*, July 6, 1922, p. 4. **Global positioning:** John Markoff, "Finding Profit in Aiding the Lost," *New York Times*, Mar. 5, 1996, p. D1. **PARC sidebar:** George Pake, "Historical Introduction" and Carlo Sequin, "An Overview," in Giuliana Lavendel, *A Decade of Research, 1970–1980: Xerox Palo Alto Research Center* (New York : R. R. Bowker Co., 1980); C. P. Thanker, et al., "Alto: A Personal Computer," in Daniel P. Siewiorek, et al., *Computer Structures: Principles and Examples* (New York: McGraw-Hill, 1982); Alan C. Kay, "Microelectronics and the Personal Computer," *Scientific American* 237 (Sept.

1977), p. 230; Walter Teitelman, "A Display Oriented Programmer's Assistant," *International Journal of Man-Machine Studies* 11 (1979), p. 157. Note: all of the above articles are reprinted in facsimile in Lavendel, *A Decade of Research, 1970–1980: Xerox Palo Alto Research Center.*

CHAPTER SIX

Colorization: "A Bright Future for Classics," *United Press International*, June 22, 1986; Jeff Wilson, "Artists Livid over Turner Color Scheme," Associated Press, Nov. 30, 1986; Gary R. Edgerton, "'The Germans Wore Gray, You Wore Blue,'" *Journal of Popular Film and Television* 27, no. 4 (Jan. 1, 2000); Leslie Bennetts, "'Colorizing' Film Classics: A Boon or a Bane?" *New York Times*, Aug. 5, 1986. **A. W. Brabham:** "Grows Colored Cotton," *Marysville (OH) Evening Tribune*, Sept. 11, 1915, p. 1; "Colored Cotton Secret Perishes with Discoverer," Associated Press, Aug. 21, 1932. **Sally Fox:** "Colored Cotton Adds a New Air of Sophistication," Associated Press, Apr. 23, 1992; Andrea Adelson, "Organic Clothing: On Backs, Not Minds," *New York Times*, Nov. 6, 1987. **Binney & Smith:** "Instructions for Making #29 Lumber Crayon," Binney & Smith Inc. records, series 6, box 14, file 6, Archives Center, National Museum of American History, Smithsonian; A. F. Kitchel, *The Story of the Rainbow* (Easton, PA: Binney & Smith, 1961). **Robert Switzer:** "New Invention 'Fires' Colors," *Oakland Tribune*, Mar. 9, 1947, p. 24A; Jon Ronson, "How the World Turned Day-Glo," *Manchester (England) Guardian*, Jan. 15, 2005; David Cay Johnston, "Robert Switzer, Co-Inventor of Day-Glo Paint, Dies at 83," *New York Times*, Aug. 29, 1997. **Charles and Ray Eames:** Charles and Ray Eames, *House: After Five Years of Living* short film (1955); Eames Demetrios, *An Eames Primer* (New York : Universe Pub., 2001); Donald Albrecht, et al., *The Work of Charles and Ray Eames: A Legacy of Invention* (New York: Harry N. Abrams with the Library of Congress and the Vitra Design Museum, 1997); Joseph Giovannini, "Soul of the Eames Machine," *New York Times*, July 8, 1999. **Edwin Land sidebar:** "Polaroid Headlights' Time is Ripe," *Fortune* 32 (Aug. 1945), p. 236; "Automobile Lights," *New York Times*, Nov. 23, 1947, p. 96; "Polarized Headlights," *Newsweek*, Dec. 1, 1947, p 36.

CHAPTER SEVEN

Banjo: "The Banjo," *New York Times*, Aug. 19, 1884, p. 4; Michael Theodore Coolen, "Senegambian Archetypes for the American Folk Banjo," *Western Folklore* 43, no. 2 (Apr. 1984), pp. 124–131; Dena J. Epstein, "The Folk Banjo: A Documentary History," *Ethnomusicology* 19, no. 3 (Sept. 1975), pp. 351–352; Jay Bailey, "Historical Origin and Stylistic Developments of the Five-String Banjo," *Journal of American Folklore* 85, no. 335 (Jan.–Mar. 1972), p. 60; Joel Chandler Harris, "The Negro and the Banjo," *The Critic and Good Literature* 29 (July 19, 1884), p. 25. **Joshua Stoddard and the calliope:** Pat Houck, "Fire-Eating Music Box," *Charleston (WV) Gazette-Mail*, Sept. 3, 1972, p. 63; "Piped Piper of Pawlet Forgotten in Music," *Idaho Falls Post-Register*, Dec. 7, 1964, p. 13; "Music by Steam," *New York Times*, Aug. 10, 1855, p. 6; "Truman Sworn In as 32nd President," *New York Times*, Jan. 20, 1949, p. 2. **Samuel Sexton:** "A Rival of the Audiophone," *New York Times*, July 12, 1881, p. 3; "A New Umbrella," *New York Times*, Sept. 17, 1884, p. 4. **Miller Reese Hutchison:** Miller Reese Hutchison," *Birmingham News*, Feb. 22, 1944, p. 11; Winifred Rothermel, "Native of Alabama with 1,000 Patents to His Credit, Has Dual Personality," *Birmingham News*, Feb. 3, 1928, p. 3; "Tells of Enabling Alexandra to

Hear," *New York Times*, Nov. 21, 1925, p. 6; "Deaf Made to Hear," *Mansfield (OH) News*, Apr. 22, 1903, p. 3. **Manuel Nunes:** "Ukelelical," *Galveston Daily News*, Sept. 7, 1922, p. 4; "Inventor of Ukelele is Dead in Honolulu," *Waterloo Evening Courier*, July 24, 1922, p. 2. **Carleen Maley Hutchins:** Marjorie Rubin, "A Housewife in New Jersey Uses Science in Making Violins," *New York Times*, Oct. 19, 1963; Harold Schonberg, "Catgut Society," *New York Times*, Sept. 6, 1964, p. X7; Paul R. Laird, "The Life and Work of Carleen Maley Hutchins," *ARS Musica Denver* 6, no. 1 (Fall 1993). **William Sidney Mount sidebar:** Gilbert Ross, liner notes, *The Cradle of Harmony* sound recording (New York: Folkways Records, 1976); "The Great Exhibition," *New York Times*, Aug. 19, 1953, p. 2.

CHAPTER EIGHT

Charles Hovey: Charles Hovey, *Magazine of Horticulture* 3 (1837), p. 246; L. H. Bailey, "Whence Came the Cultivated Strawberry," *American Naturalist* 28, no. 328 (Apr. 1894), p. 298. **Robert Nelson:** James C. Bonner, "Advancing Trends in Southern Agriculture, 1840–1860," *Agricultural History* 22, no. 4 (October 1948), p. 253. **Ephraim Wales Bull:** "The Origin of the Concord Grape," *Dunkirk Evening Observer*, Sept. 9, 1911, p. 7. **Hard wheats:** Carleton R. Ball, "The History of American Wheat Improvement," *Agricultural History* 4, no. 2 (Apr. 1920), p. 48. **Luther Burbank:** Luther Burbank, et al., *Burbank: His Methods and Discoveries and Their Practical Application* (New York; London: Luther Burbank Press, 1914–1915), p. 50; "Luther Burbank," *Lowell Sun*, June 16, 1908, p. 3; Henry Smith Williams, *Luther Burbank: His Life and Work* (New York: Hearst's International Library Co., 1915). **Jean Rosendahl:** "C. E. Rosendahl Quietly Wed Here," *New York Times*, Dec. 23, 1934; Harman W. Nichols, "Jeannie of the Golden Cob Invents 'Drip-Trap' for Corn," *United Press International*, Aug. 29, 1949; Jean W. Rosendahl, "Serving Dish for Corn on the Cob," U.S. Patent 2,585,174, May 26, 1949; William Madden, "No More Butter Fingers," Associated Press, Jan. 26, 1950. **John H. Hammond Jr.:** Corinne B. Witham, *The Hammond Castle Cookbook* (Gloucester, MA: Hammond Castle Museum, 1969); "John H. Hammond Jr. Dies, Electronics Inventor was 76," *New York Times*, Feb. 14, 1965, p. 88; "Moonlight to Order at Home of Millionaire," *Wide World*, Apr. 19, 1942; John H. Hammond Jr., "Magnetic Mixer," U.S. Patent 2,689,114, Sept. 14, 1954; John H. Hammond Jr., "Submarine Attack Computer," U.S. Patent 2,689,083, Sept. 14, 1954; "Young Hays Hammond Bids for Laurels of Edison," *Mansfield (OH) News*, Sept. 4, 1925, p. 6. **Noiseless popcorn bag:** Erskine Johnson, "In Hollywood," *Rhinelander (WI) Daily News*, Sept. 4, 1947, p. 4; "Boon for Movies," *Berkshire Evening Herald*, Oct. 24, 1946. **Charles Welch:** "Ex-Winonan Pioneered an Industry," *Winona Daily News*, Apr. 27, 1969, p. 3. **Teressa Bellissimo:** Stephen W. Bell, "Buffalo Wings," Associated Press, Nov. 6, 1986; Dan Sewell, "20,000 a Day Business," Associated Press, Nov. 22, 1977. **Natalie Hays Hammond sidebar:** Associated Press, "Natalie Hays Hammond, 25, Daughter of Inventor, Has Own Factory for Creations," *Syracuse Herald*, Dec. 19, 1930, p. 22; Irma Benjamin, "Boredom the Modern Mother of Invention," *Oakland Tribune*, Apr. 12, 1931, p 52; "Is Being Born Rich a Lucky Stroke or a Bad Break for Genius?" *Syracuse Herald*, Jan. 18, 1931, p. 3.

CHAPTER NINE

W. C. Soule: Welling C. Soule, "Improvement in Water Skates," U.S. Patent 0214234, June 1879. **Frank Hill sidebar:** John J. Morgan, "Slate-Fall Warning Device Requires 24-Year Study," *Charleston (WV) Gazette*, Jan. 29, 1950, p. 2; "Slate Fall Warning Device is

Invented by Ex-Miner," *Beckley (WV) Post-Herald*, Feb. 2, 1950, p. 6; Christopher Mark, "The Introduction of Roof Bolting to U.S. Underground Coal Mines (1948–1950)" (21st International Conference on Ground Control in Mining, West Virginia University, Morgantown, WV, Aug. 2002): 150–160. **Stanley Van Voorhees:** Stanley Van Voorhees, "Power-Driven Ski," U.S. Patent 2625229, Jan. 13, 1953; Stacy V. Jones, "Motor Skis Make Slope Climbing Easier (Safer) Than Coming Down," *New York Times*, Jan. 17, 1953. **Howard Head:** "Howard Head, Designer of Skis, Tennis Racquets, Dies," Associated Press, Mar. 4, 1991; Howard Head, office memo, Dec. 29, 1943, Howard Head Papers, collection 589, series 1, box 2, file 1; Howard Head, letter, Apr. 26, 1947, Howard Head Papers, collection 589, series 1, box 2, file 2; Inez Foley, oral history, Employee Vignettes of Howard Head and Head Ski Company, Howard Head Papers, collection 589, series 4, box 9, file 3; Chuck Powers, oral history, Employee Vignettes of Howard Head and Head Ski Company, Howard Head Papers, collection 589, series 4, box 9, file 3. **Brother Casmir Zeglen:** "Zeglen a Target," *Syracuse Herald*, Sept. 26, 1897, p. 5; "He Fears Not Bullets," *New York Times*, Oct. 2, 1897, p. 12. **Frank Richtig:** "Mystery Knives," *Nebraska State Journal*, Jun. 30, 1940, p. 29; "Clarkson Blacksmith Works on New Fisherman's Helper," *Columbus Daily Telegram*, Mar. 23, 1965, p. 7; "Blacksmith Has Own Formula for Tempering Steel," *Columbus (NE) Daily Telegram*, Jan. 26, 1961, p. 11; H. W. Paxton and J. B. Austin, "Historical Account of the Contributions of E.C. Bain," *Metallurgical Transactions* 3 (May 1972), p. 1035; Robert Ripley, "Believe It or Not," King Features Syndicate, published in *Lincoln [NE] State Journal*, November 18, 1936, p. 15; Jeffrey Wadsworth and Donald R. Lesuer, "The Knives of Frank J. Richtig . . ." *Materials Characterization* 45 (2000), p. 315; E. S. Davenport and E. C. Bain, "Transformation of Austenite at Constant Subcritical Temperatures," *Transactions AIME* 90 (1930); Edgar C. Bain and Edmund S. Davenport, "Thermally Hardening Steel," U.S. Patent 1924099, Aug. 29, 1933. **Donald Crabtree and Ishi:** "Find a Rare Aborigine," *New York Times*, Sept. 7, 1911, p. 3; Entry for obsidian scalpel, online catalog, Fine Science Tools, Inc., http://www.finescience.com/commerce/ccp4064-obsidian-scalpel---large-10110-03.htm; Don E. Crabtree, *An Introduction to Flintworking* (Pocatello: Idaho State University Museum, 1972); Don E. Crabtree, "Mesoamerican Polyhedral Cores and Prismatic Blades," *American Antiquity* 55 (1968); J. J. Disa, J. Vossoughi, and N. H. Goldberg, "A Comparison of Obsidian and Surgical Steel Scalpel Wound Healing in Rats," *Plastic and Reconstructive Surgery* 92, no. 5 (Oct. 1993), p. 887. **Tommy Glenn Carmichael:** Adam Goldman, "Slot Machine Cheat Bilked Casinos for Years with Gadgets," Associated Press, Aug. 14, 2003. **J. P. Kepplinger:** "Seventy-Five Years of Gambling History in America," *Salt Lake City Tribune*, July 19, 1914, p. 44. **Joseph Peavey sidebar:** Don Gross, "Stillwater Retains Memories of Romantic Lumbering Days," *Portland Press Herald*, July 27, 1948, p. 59; "The Loggers; or, Six Months in the Forests of Maine," *Merry's Museum for Boys and Girls* (Boston: Horace B. Fuller, 1869), p. 30–32; Louis Clinton Hatch, *Maine: A History* (New York: American Historical Society, 1919), p. 691; Peavey company Web site, www.PeaveyMfg.com. **Vest-proof bullet sidebar:** "'Bullet-Proof' Vests Riddled," *New York Times*, July 24, 1938, p. 28; Wolcott Gibbs, "Comment," *New Yorker*, Aug. 20, 1938, p. 7.

CHAPTER TEN

Father Himalaya: J. A. Graham, "Sun Motor Solves Mystery of Electricity's Source," *Chicago Tribune*, Nov. 6, 1904; "Melting Fire Clay with Sun's Rays," (Waterloo, IA) *Daily Times Tribune*, Sept. 9, 1906, p. 13; "Pyrheliophor Wonder of St. Louis Fair," *New York Times Magazine*, Nov. 6, 1904, p. SM6. **Edward Farrow:** Percy Noel, "Engineer Claims

Ability to Suppress Gravity," *Aviation Week* 3, no. 7 (Nov. 18, 1911); "How to Overcome Gravity by Hertzian Air," *New York Times Magazine*, July 16, 1911, p. 3. **Robert Goddard:** Robert Goddard, "The High Speed Bet," *Worcester Polytechnic Institute Journal* 18, no. 1 (Nov. 1914), p 12; Robert Goddard, "Vacuum Tube Transportation System," U.S. Patent 2,511979, June 20, 1950. **James Powell and Gordan Danby:** William W. Dickhart III, "The 2000 Benjamin Franklin Medal in Engineering," *Journal of the Franklin Institute* 337 (2000), p. 829; John Noble Wilford, "Researchers Cut Link to Stanford," *New York Times*, July 4, 1970, p. 19; Earl Lane, "Attractive Potential in Magnetic Trains," *Newsday*, June 7, 1975; Daniel Patrick Moynihan, "Putting Pizzazz Back in Public Works," *New York Times*, Mar. 6, 1998, p. 21; Peter Marks, "Levitating Train Faces Uphill Fight," *New York Times*, June 13, 1994. **Theodore Maiman:** Ralph Righton, "Then He Invented the Miracle Tool," Associated Press, Mar. 22, 1964; "An ABC of Light and Lasers," *New York Times*, Sept. 8, 1963, p. SM124; John Barbour, "It's Still Not a Ray-Gun," Associated Press, Nov. 5, 1995; "Death Rays Secret Nears for Science," Associated Press, Oct. 2, 1960; "Developer of the Laser Calls It 'A Solution Seeking a Problem,'" *New York Times*, May 6, 1964.

ACKNOWLEDGMENTS

The Jerome and Dorothy Lemelson Center for the Study of Invention and Innovation is one of the newest assets of the Smithsonian Institution, having been founded at the National Museum of American History in 1995. It explores the world of invention in the past, but it doesn't stop there. The Lemelson Center makes a museum of the whole nation and beyond, encouraging inventive creativity in everyone—right now, today. It has been a privilege for me to work with the people who shape the Lemelson Center's philosophy. Director Arthur Molella lent this project his strong encouragement and advice, both of which were invaluable from the start. Joyce Bedi, senior historian at the Center, located the illustrations for the book. She is not only a master of the history of invention, but a person of rare sensitivity and humor; I will be forever indebted to her.

The manuscript was reviewed by various members of the Lemelson Center staff, for which I am grateful. I remain, however, responsible for the content, facts, and opinions in the text.

The Lemelson Center works closely with the museum's Archives Center, a fast-growing repository for the papers of inventors—from doodles to reminiscences to diaries—showing not just what they invented, but also what train of thought brought a new idea to the fore. I am obliged to Alison Oswald, Lemelson Center archivist, for making my time at the Archives so productive.

Research was conducted at the following libraries, starting with the Onondaga County Public Library, which located many far-flung books and microfilms for me through the Inter-Library Loan system, New York Public Library, Library of Congress, Buffalo and Erie County Library, Boston Public Library, Syracuse University Science and Technical Library, and Princeton University Library.

At HarperCollins, I was extremely fortunate to work with Bruce Nichols, the publisher, as well as Serena Jones and Kathryn Antony, the editors of the book. I am also very much obliged to Christopher Goff. Donna Sanzone was instrumental in launching this book.

I would like to thank my father, Warren Fenster, MIT, class of 1950, for helping me with several technical issues; Richard Harfmann, for assistance at every turn; and Lillian Schwartz—Princeton, class of 2011, as long as I am waxing collegiate—who tramped the libraries with me. And always, Neddy.

Art Credits

Anchor Bar Franchise Company LLC: 152
Archives Center, National Museum of American History, Smithsonian Institution: 27, 61, 106, 107, 159, 182
Bell Laboratories, courtesy AIP Emilio Segre Visual Archives: 76, 77, 191
Becker Medical Library, Washington University School of Medicine: 125, 127
Cary Wolinski, photographer, courtesy of Vreseis Ltd. and FoxFibre®: 105
Charles Allen Herndon, "Motion Pictures by Ether Waves," *Popular Radio* 8 (August 1925: 107–113): 30
Charles Scribner's Sons Publication: 43(r)
Chemical Heritage Foundation Collections, Philadelphia, PA: 66
Christopher Schwartz © 2006: 8(b)
Derek Jensen (Tysto): 46(bl)
Dr. Henry Kolm: 187
Eigentum des jeweiligen Sutdios/Vertriebes: 99(b)
Eli Whitney Museum: 20
Fine Science Tools Inc.: 172(b)
Farnsworth Archives (http://philotfarnsworth.com): 29
Farnsworth/Everson Collection, Arizona State University: 31
Florida Center for Instructional Technology: 124
Fons Vanden Berghen Photo Collection, Halle, Belgim: 3
Glendale Community College © Stan Celestian: 172(t)
Jake Brower: 26
John Roberts © used by permission: 45(t)
Joyce Gilbert, via Eli Whitney Museum: 23
Julie M. Fenster: 167
Karen M. Schwallie: 9
Lemelson Center, National Museum of American History, Smithsonian Institution: 190
Library of Congress: 6(r), 7, 36, 40, 41, 42(t), 44(b), 47(b), 82, 83, 110, 111, 121, 123, 126, 134, 147
Manufacturer and Builder Magazine: 43(l)

M. F. Sweetser, King's Handbook of Newton (Boston: Moses King, 1899), p. 204: 143

Minnesota Historical Society: 138

National Air and Space Museum, Smithsonian Institution: 4

National Anthropological Archives, Smithsonian Institution: 170

National Museum of American History, Smithsonian Institution: 6(l), 18, 21, 22(t), 53, 57, 59, 64, 117, 178, 179

Naval Research Library: 86(r), 87

Official Gazette of the U.S. Patent Office, Aug. 7 1894, p. 684: 143

Paul Birchmeyer Auction Service: 113

Purdue University Libraries, Archives and Special Collections: 47(t)

Queens Borough Public Library, Long Island Division, Lewis H. Latimer Collection: 37

RFCGO.com: 22(b)

Robert G. Sullivan, Schenectady Digital History Archive, Schenectady County Public Library: 63

Smithsonian Institution Archives: 42(b), 44(t), 186

Smithsonian Institution Libraries: 103

Smithsonian Institution, photo by Dr. Erich Salomon: 38

Steamship Historical Society of America: 122

Strong National Museum of Play®, Rochester, NY, 5/09: 23(b)

Switzer family via Robert & Patricia Switzer Foundation: 108

T. R. Hazen, Pond Lily Mill Restorations: 139

United States Patent and Trademark Office, http://www.uspto.gov: 14, 24(b), 25

U.S. Air Force: 86(l), 88

U.S. Dept. of the Interior, National Park Service at Edison National Historic Site: 55(r), 60, 62

USDA History Collection. Special Collections, National Agriculture Library: 137

INDEX

ABOUT THE AUTHOR

J ulie M. Fenster is an award-winning author and historian, specializing in the American story. She has written the *New York Times* bestseller *Parish Priest* with Douglas Brinkley, *Ether Day*, which won the prestigious Anesthesia Foundation Award for Best Book, and *Race of the Century*, which was nominated for the Pulitzer Prize. She lives in New York.